Living Ghosts & Mischievous Monsters

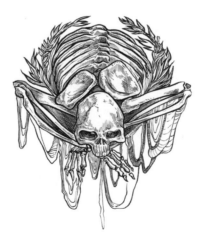

Living Ghosts & Mischievous Monsters

CHILLING AMERICAN INDIAN STORIES

Written and Selected by
DAN SASUWEH JONES
PONCA NATION

Illustrated by
WESHOYOT ALVITRE
TONGVA

SCHOLASTIC PRESS / NEW YORK

DEDICATED TO:

John Rohner,
a Master Craftsman, turning Story into Art

Produced by Potomac Global Media, LLC

Text copyright © 2021 by Dan SaSuWeh Jones

Illustrations copyright © 2021 by Weshoyot Alvitre

Library of Congress Cataloging-in-Publication Data available

ISBN 978-1-338-68162-8

10 9 8 7 6 5 4 3 2   22 23 24 25

Printed in the U.S.A.   113

First printing September 2021

Dreamscape

The hour is late,
the night is long, and it is cold,
the trail is long, and it is old.
Stories kept and stories lost,
once you read a story that filled you with hope,
and read one that filled you with loss.
But it was that one about ghosts,
that you remember the most!

Who are they and from where did they come?
Are they as old as us, are they as wise, are they even the same?
Are they the truth, or are they a lie?
Why is it that the one about ghosts,
we remember the most?

Sleep this night, and many more, until you grow old and wise.
Forget those stories of fairies, gremlins, and trolls.
Close your eyes and sleep tonight.
All is filled with hope, fear of loss is far away . . .
But that story of ghosts,
you will fear the most!

—SaSuWeh, Ponca Nation, 2020

Contents

CHAPTER FOUR: MONSTERS

CHAPTER FIVE: THE SUPERNATURAL

Introduction

Ghost stories were a big part of my life growing up as an American Indian. As a young member of the Ponca Nation of Oklahoma, I spent many evenings listening to our tribal elders tell us chilling tales. When I was older, I traveled across the country to collect stories from other tribes. Until then, I did not realize that ghost stories are held as deeply in other American Indian tribes and nations as they are in mine. Many of these stories take place long ago; some are in the recent past; and many are told as if they've just happened—because sometimes they have. Ghost stories are always close to us because ghosts are part of our daily world.

Not all things strange are ghosts. Stories of the unknown come in many shapes and forms that tell of unexplainable—sometimes horrible—things. Some are about demons or evil spirits. Others are about inanimate objects, like glowing orbs, apparitions, or even dolls that take on the breath of life. In this book, I have divided the world of American Indian ghosts into five categories: "Ghosts," "Spirits," "Witches," "Monsters," and "The Supernatural," to give a clearer, more defined picture of what you may encounter— from an unseen noise to a hideous face to maybe something no one else has ever experienced. But let me start from the beginning.

While on summer break from the University of Colorado, instead of taking my usual trip home to Oklahoma, I accepted an invitation to stay with a friend from the Colville Indian Reservation, in Washington State. His family owned a ranch with lots of extremely beautiful land that bordered tribal lands. That provided a welcome getaway from the city. They had horses, and there were trails from their land to the tribal lands, which were filled with clean rivers, lakes, and beaver ponds. You could spend weeks there and rarely see another person. My friend and I put together a tepee and a month's worth of food and headed into the wilderness. We met people living there and recorded their ghost stories. I spent the next five years crisscrossing the nation, living on American Indian lands, meeting some of the most fascinating people and collecting their stories, too.

I lived without electricity, and after dark, friends would gather for a fire-lit evening meal followed by a night of telling stories. I was fascinated by all the master storytellers I met. Their audience might never be over a hundred people in their life of storytelling. Yet they pass on stories that will live for centuries within their own cultures.

It soon became clear across all the regions I traveled that there was one type of common, recurring story—the ghost story. This became my umbrella term for the stories about all the things that frighten people the most: ghosts and monsters and witches and other unknown beings that live all around us.

Years later, when I began compiling my stories, they seemed to fall into categories—not scientific in any way; just natural. Each is a chapter in this book, and at the beginning of each chapter, I will define these different types for you and explain their importance to American Indian cultures.

I hope you'll enjoy what I learned in my travels throughout Indian America. At the top of each story I've included information so you'll know where that tale came from. You'll see my byline next to my own ghost encounters, both during my travels and at home among my Ponca tribe. I have also included some ancient stories to show the differences between types of stories and cultures through time. Other stories I collected from authors today. I am deeply grateful to the storytellers I met in person and to all the other authors who contributed to this book. Some tribal cultures are not allowed to share certain ghost stories because the spirits are so real to them that saying the spirit names may endanger the storytellers and their families—I respect that, and I did not include those stories.

Of the many stories from Indian America, this collection just scratches the surface. But the stories are real, and they have kept many young listeners awake late into the night . . .

—*Dan SaSuWeh Jones*

CHAPTER ONE

Ghosts

A ghost is a form of energy. In life, that energy is in the form of a person, an animal, or any other being. When that being dies, the energy takes on a new form, as a ghost. Ghosts are mostly associated with an event, usually a tragic moment when a life is lost suddenly. The heart stops beating in this world, but the sound of the beating heart remains, leaving a bit of the energy among us. The rest of the energy transfers to a spiritual plane. Generally, ghosts appear around the place of the tragic event, and they relive it repeatedly. Usually this energy is angry because it feels trapped. It is looking for a way out. Many cultures believe that ghosts are not here to harm us, while others consider them dangerous. In my experience, they have little to no physical effect on the living—unless someone hurts themselves when reacting to a ghost! Indeed, some ghosts may carry a message that can save lives or warn people of trouble. While less frequent, the ghosts of animals may also relive the tragic event that took their life. In the end, of all possible otherworldly events, ghost encounters are the least dangerous. Sometimes ghosts are confused with spirits—but they are just one kind of spirit. And many other spirits have far more complex agendas, as we'll find out in Chapter Two.

My Great-Aunt's Last Ten A.M. Visit

TOLD BY DAN SASUWEH JONES, PONCA

*It is an old belief of the Ponca, my tribe, that after a person passes
away, they come back for a last visit to all their relatives.
While we may not see them, or they may appear only in our dreams,
they let us know they have come.*

W e lived in the country far from town, but members of our
extended family had homes nearby. One was my great-aunt
Agnes. She had lost her husband many years before my time
and she was quite elderly, but still active. Almost every day that weather
permitted, she would walk from her house to our home, a distance of
about a quarter mile, or three blocks by city measure. It was her daily
exercise and maybe the reason she had lived so long. We knew when
she'd gotten to our house because she always came in the door of the
screened-in porch. You could hear the old screen door make a creaking
sound as it opened and its spring was pulled taut, followed by the slam
as it closed hard.

Aunt Agnes would walk the few steps across the old board floor to the
back door of our kitchen. She had a very distinctive walk with a limp—
she walked heavier on one side, with a louder footstep than on the other
side. While she made her way across the old porch floorboards, her steps

were amplified, and from about anywhere in the house you could hear her entering. She would always visit at midmorning, around ten a.m. You could set your clock by her visit. When Mom would first hear the screen door stretching its spring, she would yell out, "Go help your aunt Agnes open the back door." And my father or one of us kids would run to the back door to let her in.

My great-aunt Agnes was a historian of our tribe, and she would spend about an hour with my mother on each of her visits, telling her about our heritage. Mom always had water on the stove to boil and would make tea for the two of them. After her visit, Aunt Agnes would be off, back to her home. Mom would offer her a ride, but Aunt Agnes would always refuse it and say that the walk did her good.

It had been a few days since Aunt Agnes's last visit, but the weather had been bad, with rain and storms in the late morning and afternoon, so it wasn't of any concern to us. During that time my father had started to replace some of the old boards on the back porch. He had cut the boards to length and set them in place, but he hadn't nailed them all down. One of those stormy mornings, my mother and sister and I were sitting in the dining room when we all heard the spring on the screen door being pulled taut as it opened.

My mother said, "It must be your father working on that floor."

"No, Mom," my sister replied. "He went after some nails in town."

Then my mother turned as white as a sheet, thinking her aunt had come for a visit and may have fallen through the loose boards. She sat straight up.

"It's your aunt Agnes. Go help her!"

We all heard the old boards creaking and Aunt Agnes's signature limp moving to the kitchen door. Mom and my sister were up in a flash, and I followed behind them as Mom began to open the door. Then she turned to us with a look of relief, as my aunt was nowhere in sight. "That was strange," Mom said. "I swore I heard her!"

That's when there was a loud knock on our front door. It was my cousin

Susan, who had clearly been crying. When my mother asked her what was wrong, Susan said words that I still remember to this day: "Dear Aunt Agnes. They found her dead early this morning. She died in her sleep."

At that moment it was ten a.m.

The Mashpee Sailor

BASED ON A TRADITIONAL WAMPANOAG TALE, MASSACHUSETTS,
TOLD BY SAMANTHA HATCH

*For twelve thousand years the Mashpee have lived on Cape Cod,
Massachusetts, surrounded by the Atlantic Ocean. Their name means
"Large Water." Part of the big Wampanoag Nation, they were among the
first Indians to meet European settlers in the 1600s. The Mashpee made
a living fishing and trading along the coast, so seafarers and fishermen
were familiar sights in a Mashpee village. Life changed after the
Europeans came, but Mashpee values of hospitality and family ties
remained strong. In this story a ghost returns to the realm of the living to
test the generosity and loyalty of a young mother. Will she pass his test?*

I t was a cool night near the Cape, and the young mother sat in her
wigwam knitting a blanket late into the night. It was hours until
she would sleep, for she had much work to do. She would sell the
blanket to feed her two children, for her handiwork was all she had to
trade. The children's father had been lost to illness two winters ago.

Her door flap was wide open in a welcoming gesture, as was custom-
ary of her people, and maybe it was just the wind that made her look up,
or maybe it was a different kind of chill. When she looked outside, she
saw a man standing there in the dark.

"Hello?" she said. "Is someone there?" The fog was thick this night,
and it seemed to somehow billow more thickly around the dark figure.

The figure stepped closer, and she was no longer afraid. He had a kind

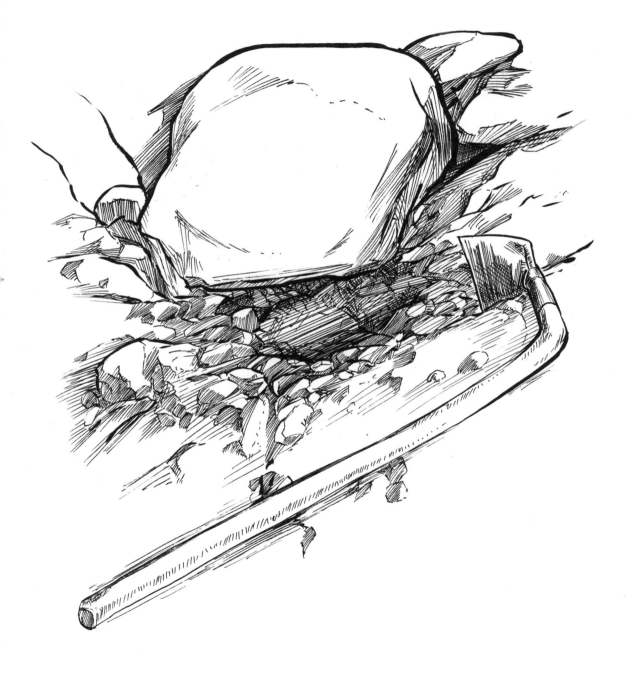

face and wore a sailor's clothing, the kind her people wore, though it looked a little worse for wear.

"May I warm myself by your fire?" the sailor asked. "My clothes are wet and I have traveled far this day."

She invited him inside and added another log to the fire. As the stranger sat, she returned to her knitting. After a few moments, she glanced at the man sitting near the fire, and that is when she saw it. She could see the fire right through his legs. As if he were made of the mist that had surrounded him outside. She realized, with a jolt, that this was no man. He was a ghost!

The young mother was brave and showed no fear. He had not threatened her with harm. She glanced quickly over her shoulder at her sleeping children to see that they were safe, then returned to her knitting, keeping a close eye on the ghost. They sat in silence for several minutes before he spoke.

"I see that you are not a rich woman," the ghost said.

The young mother said nothing, for it was not a question.

"I see that you have little," he continued, "but you have helped me this night. If you would like a large pot full of gold, you will find one buried behind your wigwam, near a large rock. It will be enough to keep you for many years to come."

And with that, the ghost stood and left her home.

The young mother shivered. It was not until he was gone that she noted the extra chill in the air that the ghost had brought with him. She waited a few minutes, tucking the blankets tighter around her little ones while she waited. She wanted to be sure that the ghost was gone before she considered what to do.

After a few long moments, thoughts of the gold crept into her mind. She needed money to buy food and new clothes for her children.

The mother took her hoe and walked out and around to the back of her wigwam. There, as the ghost had said it would be, was a large rock sitting beside a patch of freshly dug earth. She began to dig. As she did, she heard her daughter cry out. She ran around to the door of her home to check on the child. But her daughter was sound asleep, the blankets undisturbed.

The young mother was confused, for she was sure that she'd heard her daughter scream. Again she walked around to the back of the wigwam and began to dig. With each strike of the ground with her hoe, she heard a child cry as if in pain. This time it sounded like her young son. She dropped her hoe and ran around the wigwam.

But she was wrong again. Her son lay quietly next to his sister, sound asleep.

One more time she returned to the site of the large rock and the promised riches. She picked up her hoe and began to dig. This time she heard them both, clear as they could be, screaming as if something was hurting them, killing them! Dropping the hoe, she ran inside.

Again, she found them sleeping.

Trembling, she had to clear her mind of the memory of the screams. She climbed into the bed with her children, pulled them close, and emptied her mind of their cries and the pot full of gold. She slept.

In the morning, she woke with the sun. She wondered if last night's visitor had been a dream. After dressing her children and giving them breakfast, she ventured out into the cool gray morning. As she reached the spot where she'd left her hoe the night before, she knew it wasn't a dream. Near the large rock was a deep, round hole. The earth had been dug up, and whatever buried treasure had been there was long gone. She had no time to lament this before she heard a woman scream.

This scream did not come from her home. Instead it came from far away. Still, the sound was unmistakable—an earsplitting shriek of grief.

She dressed her children warmly and they joined the other villagers running toward the sound. When they arrived, the mother learned that a woman had awakened to find her child dead. It was her shriek the mother had heard piercing the morning. The villagers had tried to comfort the woman, but she'd run toward the cliffs.

They had tried, but they had failed. The mist swallowed her forever.

Near her bed the villagers found a dirt-covered hoe and a chest over-flowing with gold coins.

The young mother never forgot that cold night or her ghostly visitor. She held her children close to her and they lived for many years. They never had riches, but they were happy having one another.

You Don't Live Here Anymore

Told by Herman Viola, Smithsonian National Museum of the American Indian

*In 1972, while I was the director of the National Anthropological
Archives at the Smithsonian's National Museum of Natural History,
I started a program for Indian communities to build their own tribal
archives. One of my first interns was David Fanman Sr. from the
Southern Cheyenne tribe in Oklahoma. We became close friends, and
several times I visited his reservation and his successful tribal archive.
I also came to know his son, David Fanman Jr. David Jr. was proud to
be a Cheyenne, but he did not share the spiritual beliefs of a traditional
Indian. One day I asked him: "Hasn't anything spiritual ever happened
to you?" He replied: "Well, I had one experience that I still can't
understand and explain, and since you asked, I will tell you."
Here's David Jr.'s story in his words.*

A few years back my younger brother Jim was killed in a car accident near our home in Canton, Oklahoma.

On the day of the funeral and burial, our whole family was at home, sitting silently. My mother and some of my sisters were crying. We were looking at photographs. Sometimes one of us would speak up with a memory.

Suddenly, our dogs started barking. Then they raced down the hill to the road that runs along our property.

We all figured a car was coming because the dogs always did that when one came up the hill to our house.

"It must be friends of Jim who want to pay their respects," Dad said to us. "I know you don't want to talk to anyone, but please be polite. These visitors mean well and they are coming in honor of your brother."

We all nodded as we wiped the tears from our faces. We stood up to prepare to greet the guests.

Within a few minutes we could hear the dogs barking as they returned up the hill. We listened for the car engine. Nothing. Then one of my sisters went to a window to see who was coming.

Suddenly, she yelled out, "Daddy, there is no car! What are the dogs barking at?"

Dad stood up, frowning. Then he let out a sigh and starting walking toward the door. "I was worried this would happen," he said to us. "It is your brother. He thinks he still lives here."

We all looked at one another. How could he possibly know that?

As Dad went outside, all of us kids gathered at the windows and watched. My mother stood on the porch, her handkerchief to her eyes.

Dad walked out to the little rise where the road met our front walk. The dogs stopped barking and came to sit quietly next to him.

Dad smiled sadly as he spoke to the air in front of him, waving his arms and hands as he would do when talking in sign language. Then he stopped, put his hands to his sides, and nodded again to the air.

He stood there awhile. It looked as if he were watching someone walk back down the hill. On the porch, our mother was crying again.

After a few minutes, Dad turned around and headed slowly up, onto the porch. Taking my mother's hand, he walked with her back into the house.

"What happened?" We all gathered around our parents.

"Yes," he said, "that was your brother. I told him we loved him and would never forget him, but he had to join the spirit world. I told him, 'You don't live here anymore.'"

The Lame Warrior
and the Skeleton

TRADITIONAL ARAPAHO TALE, OKLAHOMA, TOLD BY LITTLE-CHIEF, ARAPAHO

The Arapaho are legendary for their skill as horsemen. In the 1700s and 1800s, long after Europeans had introduced horses to North America, Arapahos galloped across the Great Plains of Colorado and Wyoming to hunt buffalo and wage war. But in earlier times, the Arapaho traveled on foot. A spiritual people, their world revolved around the land where they grew crops and hunted. A hunting party would pursue a herd of buffalo on foot, with bow and arrow. Once they had killed a creature, the hunters took care to give thanks to the animal and to their Creator, Be He Teiht. Deep respect and admiration for elders has always led young Arapaho warriors to build successful lives following in their elders' footsteps, even becoming great chiefs.

I n the days before horses, a party of young Arapahos set off on foot one autumn morning in search of wild game in the western mountains. They carried heavy packs of food and spare moccasins, and one day as they were crossing the rocky bed of a shallow stream, a young warrior felt a sudden sharp pain in his ankle. The ankle swelled and the pain grew worse until they pitched camp that night.

Next morning the warrior's ankle was swollen so badly that it was impossible for him to continue the journey with the others. His

companions decided it was best to leave him. They cut young willows and tall grass to make a thatched shelter for him, and after the shelter was finished, they collected a pile of dry wood so that he could keep a fire burning.

"When your ankle gets well," they told him, "don't try to follow us. Go back to our village and await our return."

After several lonely days, the lame warrior tested his ankle, but it was still too painful to walk on. And then one night a heavy snow fell, virtually imprisoning him in the shelter. Because he had been unable to kill any wild game, his food supply was almost gone.

Day by day he grew weaker. Then late one afternoon he looked out and saw a large herd of buffalo rooting in the snow for grass quite close to his shelter. He reached for his bow and arrow, then shot the fattest one and killed it.

He crawled out of the shelter to the buffalo and gave thanks to Be He Teiht.

Little by little he skinned the animal and brought in the meat. After preparing a bed of coals, he placed a section of ribs in the fire for roasting.

Night had fallen by the time the ribs were cooked, and just as the lame warrior was reaching for a piece to eat, he heard footsteps crunching on the frozen snow. The steps came nearer and nearer to the closed flap of the shelter.

"Who can that be?" he said to himself. "I am here alone and unable to run, but I shall defend myself if need be." He reached for his bow and arrow.

A moment later the flap opened and there stood a skeleton. It was wearing a tanned robe pinned tight at the neck so that only the skull was visible above. Sticking out from the robe below were its skeleton feet. It looked down at the lame warrior.

"Who are you?" cried the warrior as he hid his eyes in fright.

"You must not be frightened of me," the skeleton said in a hoarse voice.

"I have taken pity on you. Now you must take pity on me. Give me a piece of those roast ribs to eat, for I am very hungry."

Still alarmed by the presence of this unexpected visitor, the warrior sat up straight and offered a large piece of meat to the bony hand that came toward him. He was astonished to see the skeleton chew the food with its bared teeth and swallow it.

"I am the one who gave you the pain in your ankle," said the skeleton. "I am the one who caused your ankle to swell so that you could not continue on the hunt. I did it for a reason. If you had gone on with your companions, you would have been killed."

It continued in its low voice: "The day they left you here, an enemy war party made a charge upon them, and they were all killed. I am the one who saved your life."

Now the young warrior looked up at him. "Thank you, Father," he said with respect. "I am grateful to be here."

Again the skeleton's bony hand reached out, this time to rub the warrior's ankle. The pain and swelling vanished at once.

"Now you can walk again," the ghost said. "Your enemies are all around, but follow me. I will lead you safely back to your village."

At dawn they left the shelter and started off across the snow. The skeleton led the way.

All day long they walked—through deep woods, along icy streams, and over high hills. Late in the afternoon the skeleton led the warrior up a steep ridge.

When they reached the summit, the warrior gazed down into the valley below. There he saw the smoke of tepees in his Arapaho village.

With grateful eyes, he turned to his companion, promising to protect his people as the ghost had protected him.

But his companion had vanished, leaving only an icy wind in its wake.

The Dark Figure

Told by Stephanie Slim, Navajo, Arizona

I grew up on the Navajo Reservation with deeply rooted culture and traditions. My childhood was full of stories of skinwalkers and ghosts, and hearing testimony of my family members' encounters with them. A skinwalker is usually a healer who transforms at night—maybe into a coyote or wolf—and uses his good powers to do evil work. Ghosts can take many forms and visit in many ways, sometimes even following us from place to place. As an adult I now live off the reservation, but I return to my homeland once or twice a month to check on my hogan. I usually bring my dog, too. My dog is my security. She barks more during my stay, but it's normal, considering all the wildlife living out there in the wilderness. This time was different.

It was last summer. I went to bed as usual. I often leave my battery-operated lamp on at night because it's very dark inside—day or night. My hogan is a roundish structure made of mud. It only has one window and no electricity or running water.

My dog usually wakes me up in the middle of the night when she needs to go outside, but this time she didn't. I just happened to wake up and turn to my side to face the woodstove at the center of my hogan. That's when I saw it.

Someone was standing behind the woodstove—a dark figure shaped like a person. I watched it for a few seconds; then it seemed to notice me,

almost as if we made eye contact . . . except it didn't have any eyes. It shifted slightly.

I needed a brain check. I shut my eyes to make sure I was really awake. When I reopened them, the dark figure was evaporating into the ceiling, rushing out through the opening for the woodstove pipe.

Whoosh! I quickly closed my eyes because I could feel its wind against my face as it left. It felt like someone fanning me with feathers. I must have fallen back to sleep immediately afterward.

I didn't have time to question what I saw until I woke up later that morning. I had no doubt in my mind that I had seen something. I wanted to believe it was an angel, but it was dark—and angels aren't dark.

I now believe it was a ghost.

My dog didn't even bark or go outside that night—she stayed deep asleep. Years before, my mother, who lived alone at the time, would tell me she heard tapping on her wall at night, and her dogs would bark and cry. A healer/medicine man had told her that a ghost would come into her house when she was asleep—a ghost sent by a living someone to spy on her. Now, I believed, that ghost was coming to spy on me and my family.

After seeing this dark figure, I became more aware of my surroundings, and I watched for it again. I didn't see it in my hogan at Christmas break, but when I got back to my house in the city with my family, things started falling, mostly in my daughter's room. A blessing feather that was tightly secured to her bedroom wall lay on the floor one afternoon. I picked it up and put it back, only to return a few minutes later to see it on the floor again. In the middle of the night I would wake up to crashing noises as toys and other objects fell off the shelves.

One night I was sleeping with my daughter in her room. Suddenly, I felt a poke—like a finger, or maybe my dog's nose waking me up to let her out. But nothing was there. I didn't want to alarm my family, so I kept it to myself.

Then my daughter started to be scared at night—even with the lights

22

on. She knew nothing of what I was experiencing. But I believe she was feeling the presence of the ghost.

I had to do something.

I asked my sister to send me some cuttings of cedar and ash trees from the homeland. When they arrived, I burned them to release their medicinal properties. By smudging my house with their smoke, I could cleanse and protect it from bad spirits.

"You must leave!" I said to the thing in my house.

The smudging worked for a while. I even made two visits back to the reservation with no problem. But after the second visit, things started going wrong again. The lights in the city house would be on when I came home, even though I knew I'd turned them off as I left. In the garage, my car alarm, which never goes off, would start honking out of nowhere. And the garage door kept getting stuck—even after someone came to fix it.

The garage! I thought. I hadn't smudged it with the rest of the house. I immediately smudged it with cedar smoke, and that's been the end of the problems—for now.

Somehow, I believe, a ghost attached to me or my daughter. Was it the same dark figure I saw in my hogan that summer? Was it the same ghost that had haunted my mother? Will it come again? I don't know.

All I can say is I have no fear of it. My prayers keep me strong for my family and myself.

The Boy Who Watched Over the Children

TOLD BY DAN SASUWEH JONES, PONCA

Chilocco Indian Agricultural School, a boarding school on the Oklahoma-Kansas border, was established in 1880 by the United States government. Its mission was to separate American Indian children from their tribes, families, and cultures. Children from tribes across the United States were brought there to learn the American way of life and leave behind their traditional beliefs and values, including changing their native languages to English and their native religions to Christianity. Then they would not know how to carry on their tribal traditions. Sometimes, however, the culture does not die with its people but is passed on in dreams and through the spirit world. And the spirit never dies.

I am an artist who makes sculptures. In 2019, several tribes hired me to build a memorial at the abandoned American Indian boarding school Chilocco. Like a small city, the school and surrounding buildings once educated and housed American Indian children who were brought from reservations across America.

The school was established in 1880, soon after what was called the Indian Wars era. From the 1890s to the 1930s, the school kept records of more than a hundred children who died there and were buried at the

graveyard because it was too far to send them home. The records included each child's name, age, tribe, and when and how they died. Many died of illness, a couple died by drowning, and a few froze trying to walk home. For others, no cause of death was listed. Some say they died of a broken heart. One child was just four years old, most were grade-school age, and a few were teenagers.

The first day I went to the cemetery with my building crew, we marked off the boundaries for the monument for the children buried there and started digging the foundation. First, we would pour a cement pad, which would take several days to harden. Then we would place the monument on top.

The first night after working at the cemetery, I began to have a dream.

The dream always started the same way. While I was working at the memorial, a child would come up to me and begin speaking to me in a language I didn't understand. He was dressed from another time in American history. I wasn't afraid, just mesmerized by the boy and his strange language.

Then I noticed there were more children behind him. I couldn't see how many because they disappeared into a fog. The boy spoke again, and I struggled to understand him. Then I tried to talk with him.

"Are you lost?" I asked him. "Where are you from?" He just stared back at me, not understanding my words.

Then the boy started walking backward, away from me, still looking at me. All the children were walking away from me, too, until they disappeared into the fog. I looked around, and my crew was still working.

I yelled over to them, "Did you guys see those kids?"

"No, boss," they called back. "We didn't see any kids!"

"I'm dreaming," I told myself. I started working again. With each shovel of dirt, I dug a little deeper into the ground. Suddenly, I hit wood. As I cleared the dirt away, I saw that I had uncovered a casket.

I yelled to my crew members, "We can't put the memorial here—this is a graveyard!"

When I looked up, instead of my crew, I was surrounded by the children—of all different ages—looking at me. The same boy came right up to me and again spoke in a language I couldn't understand. Now I recognized it as American Indian, but I couldn't tell which it was of the hundreds of American Indian languages across the continent.

Then a tall boy, the oldest of all the children, spoke to me: "Do you know what he said?" I shook my head.

"He asked you if you could help him go home."

Then, one by one, the children started asking if I could take them home. I now understood them clearly. That's when the older boy, who was now carrying a baby, spoke up to the children.

"Don't bother the man." He shook his head. "He can't take us home."

The children all gathered around the older boy. I watched him hand the infant to a young girl. The way he touched their heads was so loving, and it seemed to calm them. They lifted their eyes to him, and their expressions of sadness melted. I could clearly see he was the one who watched out for all these children.

I said to him, "You are the children who are buried here, aren't you?" He looked at me with a longing and gentleness that removed the fear I felt. He didn't answer me, but I knew.

He gathered the children, and they all started walking away from me, into the fog. That's when I woke up. I had this dream every night that we worked at the cemetery.

Back on the job, it was finally the day to pour the concrete pad. Generally, I like to wait on the job site as the concrete hardens, to make sure the wet cement is protected. But by the time we were finished, the sun had gone down. The concrete was still wet, but we were so tired we decided to leave for the night.

The next day we got to the job site to check on the concrete. I was at my truck unloading when one of the crew yelled out: "Boss, you got to come see this!"

I dropped what I was doing and walked over to the cement pad. To my total amazement, the concrete was covered in footprints!

"Look!" said another worker. "They are all little children—except this one."

He pointed to a much larger print, maybe that of a teenager. There was only one of those larger prints on the pad, as if an older boy had stepped in for a moment, perhaps to pull a small child off the wet concrete. The boy who watched over the children.

CHAPTER TWO

Spirits

All spirits are connected with the Great Spirit, called the Great Mystery by some. The Ponca tribal term is *WakoNda*. (Yes, the *Black Panther* comics likely borrowed the word from us!) Literally, the term means God, and was long ago explained as "the day that follows the night; that which creates movement in all things." The Great Spirit creates a perfect balance in the universe—all based on movement and shared energy. Look at the sun as it rises and sets, and look at the Earth's constant orbit around the sun. We believe that all things move in perfect circles, such as the one-year cycle from spring to winter, and the circle of life, death, and rebirth. This movement reflects the Great Spirit's perfect energy in its infinite wisdom and power. We also believe that the Great Spirit came before all things, then all other spirits—such as ghosts—came from it. Everything contains a spirit—each river, tree, rock, building, insect, dog, and human. A spirit can change form, but it can never be destroyed. If a spirit changes, perhaps through death, its energy first moves back into the Great Spirit who created it; then it returns in another form—sometimes good, sometimes evil. In my experience, unlike ghosts, evil spirits can harm people. Perhaps a rock spirit waits to attack a passerby, or an undead woman tries to take you to replace the children she killed in a fury. Without evil, we would not appreciate good or strive to be better ourselves. That is a mystery we cannot fully understand. But in our stories, we respect it.

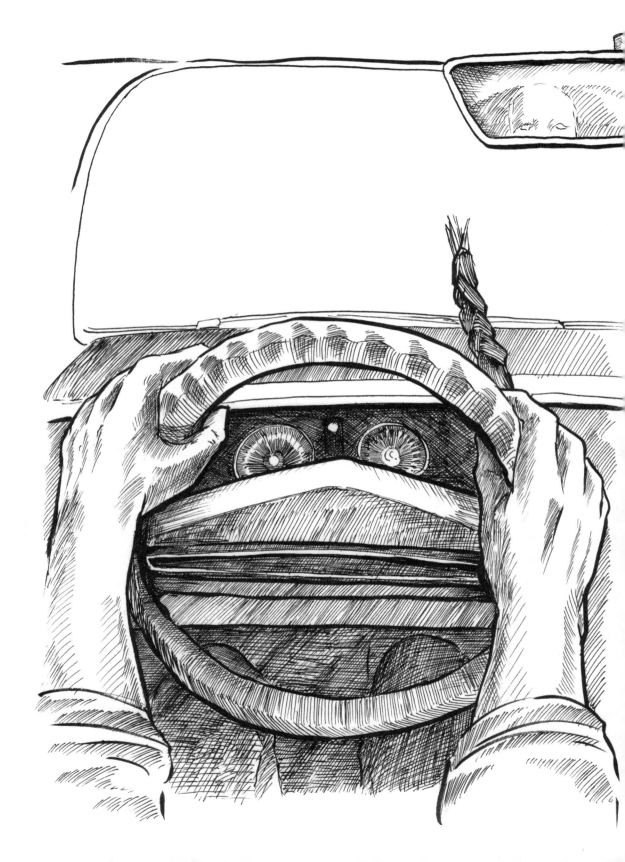

Twin Child Was Arapaho

TOLD BY MAGGIE MARIE MILLER, NORTHERN ARAPAHO, OGLALA SIOUX, WYOMING

*To save time as I drive from Laramie, Wyoming, to visit my family in
Fort Collins, Colorado, I often take a shortcut that leads through an
ancient battlefield. Here Indian ancestors, perhaps of today's Arapaho
and Sioux, once fought each other in bloody wars. I have always felt
safe driving through this area. And I always carry sweetgrass,
our traditional plant that purifies and protects us from evil spirits.
But my uncle, who is a medicine man, told me never to go
through that place at night. Now I know why.*

My five-year-old twins and I were driving from Wyoming to Colorado, just the three of us. It was late, but we had less than an hour to reach our destination, and I wanted to keep driving. One twin was sleeping, and the other was watching videos on her tablet. I usually take an alternate route during our numerous trips, which they never did like passing through at night. When I'd ask them why, they'd say, "You know why, Mommy," and look at me as if I should understand the reason.

I knew the area was once a battleground where Indian enemies fought each other, and many people were killed and buried here. But that was long ago. Today, it is a quiet, deserted, rocky stretch through the Laramie Mountains. At night you might hear an animal call or see shadows shifting, but nothing more. Besides, the route cut off so much time,

33

and tonight the girls didn't seem to be paying attention. So, I thought, *OK . . . we will be fine. I have sweetgrass on the dashboard to keep away spirits.*

We were almost halfway through the shortcut when the twin who was awake started screaming. I slammed on the brakes as she threw her tablet down and was fighting to get out of her car seat, calling for me to help her.

"Mommy!" she screamed. "There's too many, Mommy! I'm scared! Get me out now!"

"Hold on, baby," I shouted back. "I'm pulling over!"

"No! Don't stop, Mommy! Just get me out—now!"

I slowed down just enough to reach back and unbuckle her, and she jumped like a shot into the front seat.

"Buckle up!" I ordered.

"Mommy!" she cried. "Hold the sweetgrass, Mommy, and pray!"

Grasping the sweetgrass over the steering wheel, I started praying out loud. I prayed to my grandmother and grandfather, to all our ancestors. "Protect us," I called to them.

Every so often I'd glance over. My daughter was glued to the window, looking up to the sky, shaking.

Then I remembered my great-great-grandmother. She and her twin sister were the only survivors of the Sand Creek Massacre in Colorado. Like my two little girls, she, too, had been a twin. And she had seen spirits all throughout her life—good and terrible.

"What is it?" I asked frantically, between prayers.

"They're going up into the sky now, see!" she cried. "There were just too many of them, Mommy, so I got scared!"

"Too many what?" I asked. "I didn't see anything!"

"Those spirits! There were a lot, Mommy, but they went back to the sky—but keep holding the sweetgrass and praying till we get there, OK?"

"Watch over us, grandparents," I prayed again, and she started to calm down. "Tell me what they looked like," I said.

"They were riding next to us on horses and they were painted with all different colors. They had long hair. They wanted us to come with them."

Then she asked for her tablet. She had thrown it down onto the floor of the back seat, so I told her I had to stop the car to look for it.

"No! Mommy!" Her voice was still shaking. "Don't stop. Just give me your phone."

I had no internet connection, so she started clicking through my saved videos and pictures. Soon she stopped at the pictures of different moccasins. "Mommy," she said, "Mommy, look at these moccasins."

I glanced over. "Yes, I need to make you girls some moccasins, so I saved those for ideas."

She was silent for a moment, then she said, "Oh. I used to have some that looked like these, but mine were Arapaho ones." She lifted the screen to show me a pair of the beaded leather shoes.

"No, baby," I said. "Yours were Oglala Sioux moccasins that your uncle made for you."

She looked up at me, frowning. "No, Mommy, not those ones—I'm talking about the ones I used to wear when I was alive before. They were Arapaho because I was Arapaho."

I thought for a moment: That was nothing to be concerned about. I said, "You have both Sioux and Arapaho ancestors, baby."

She replied, "Yes, I know, but I was *only* Arapaho *then*."

Then she got quiet and started watching videos again.

I didn't know what to say. But I don't take that shortcut through the battlefield at night anymore.

The Deer Hunter

TOLD BY DAN SASUWEH JONES, PONCA, WHILE VISITING THE RIVER PEOPLE

Our Ponca elders have long taught us that our present is connected to our past and to our future. They have also taught us to read signs that might tell us about the future. We believe that animals such as deer communicate with one another not by sounds alone but by sight and by a silent language. The spirit world, our culture says, also communicates with us by signs. Sometimes the signs are so obvious that they stop us in our tracks and make us carefully consider our future actions.

My friend Sonny and I were young men, hunting for the tribe. We fed many families, some too old to hunt and some too young. It's not like the tribe paid us to do this—it's something all young men do. It's how we're taught: You take care of those who have a hard time taking care of themselves. It's what makes a tribe work.

One summer I was a guest of Sonny and his tribe—who called themselves the River People—far from my own tribe. For the six months I lived with them, I camped on their wooded land near their home. They treated me as their own.

Sonny's best friend was Sam. The two grew up together and shared hundreds of hunting stories. Sam lived across the reservation with his own family but was related to Sonny's family and spent a good deal of time there when he and Sonny weren't hunting.

Once Sonny introduced us, Sam and I became friends right off, and

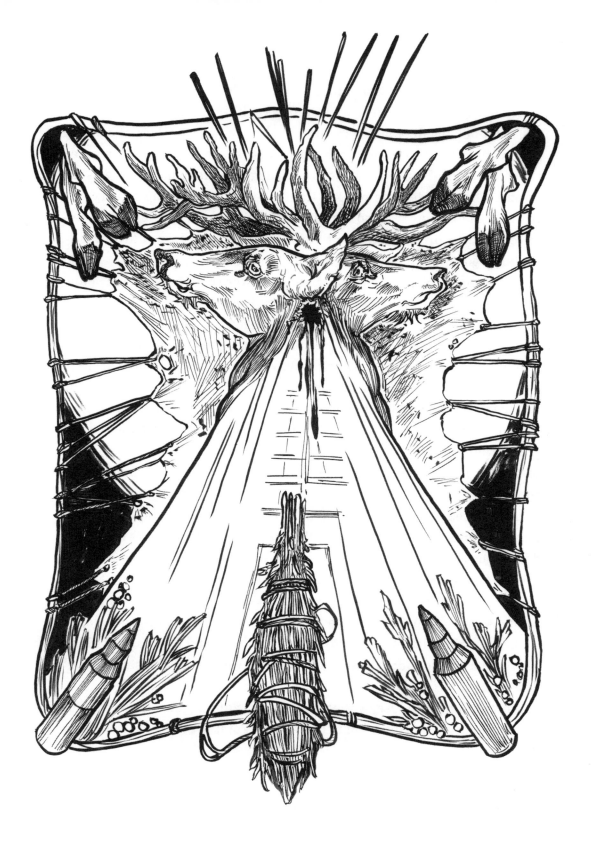

many times it was just Sam and me who would go out hunting. We had to be very careful what deer we would take. If we delivered to the elders the meat of a big deer, like a healthy buck with large antlers, the elders would chastise us. The big deer were breeders, so the old folks wanted them left alone. Besides, the meat was tough and its wild flavor was too strong. They wanted the weaker animals—the very young or very old. It was an ideal way to keep herds healthy. So we always hunted in balance with nature, no different than the way wolves would hunt. It required good judgment on the hunter's part.

It was one of those times when Sam and I were both looking at a young deer well within range. I was lying flat and so was he. I looked over my shoulder at him to confirm that this was indeed the right animal to take, and he gave me a nod. I always said a prayer as I sighted in on the animal and controlled my breathing. I was aiming just below its ear, high on its neck. If the bullet was true, it would be an instant-kill shot—no suffering; the animal would not even know it was hit. In another second I squeezed the trigger, and with a loud explosion the deer folded, dropping straight to the ground, a perfect shot! I turned to Sam, who appeared to still be holding his rifle at the ready, and I said, "Got him, a clean shot."

Sam looked at me, puzzled, saying, "I didn't hear you shoot, but I got him." I was as puzzled as he was: "I didn't hear *you* shoot," I said. As we drove our truck to pick up the deer, we argued. When we reached the deer, we paused and both said a prayer for the animal's spirit and in thanks for its sacrifice. Then we looked carefully and found two entrance wounds—one almost exactly on top of the other. "What are the odds of that happening?" Sam said, astounded. I added, "And the reason I didn't hear you and you didn't hear me is because we shot at the same time." The exact same time!

Back at Sonny's house, we cut up the deer. Sam divided some meat for Sonny's family, then drove off to deliver most of it to other tribal families he knew needed the food.

The next morning, I saw Sonny drive up to my camp and I went out to meet him. "Morning, Sonny, how about a cup of coffee?" He didn't get out of his truck and his head was down. When he looked up to me, his eyes were bloodred. He had been crying.

"What's wrong, Sonny?"

I wasn't ready for his words: "Sam was in a wreck last night, and he . . . he didn't make it. I'll be with his family for the next few days. Sam would want you to come to his funeral. I'll come back for you when it's time. You'll be ready?"

"Yes," I replied, "of course, Sonny, if there is anything I can do, just let me know, OK? And, Sonny, I'm so sorry." Sonny left to be with his friends and relatives. All that day I couldn't help but think of the incident Sam and I had had with the deer. Was it related in any way? If so, in what way?

Later that evening I decided to walk over to the main house, where Sonny and his family lived. It was a good half mile through the woods, but it was a clear, warm night with just enough moonlight to see pretty well. I wanted the time to think, and I needed to understand how this terrible thing had happened. Maybe the family had more information by now.

When I reached the house, Sonny's truck had returned from Sam's house. I went inside, and immediately I sensed something was very wrong—even beyond Sam's tragic death. The few people I saw were the oldest members of Sonny's family, and a look of shock filled their faces.

Then I heard it: A violent sound coming from down the hallway. Loud banging. Someone screaming. Sonny?

As I walked toward Sonny's room, his door opened, and his grand-mother stood in the doorway. What I saw behind her I will never forget as long as I live: Sonny on his bed, screaming, in violent convulsions. He was being bent in half from the waist and raised up from the bed to a sitting position, then slammed back down on the bed at a speed that was impossibly fast—again and again—shaken like a rag doll by a powerful force.

As his grandmother exited the room, she laid her hand directly on my chest, moving me backward while closing the door behind her. "Oh no, dear, oh no, you have to leave here, you shouldn't be here now."

"Yes, I need to go!" I said. As I turned and headed to the front door, his grandmother grabbed my hand and placed something in it. Outside I saw that it was cedar and sage, tied in a small bundle. On the front porch a couple of family members had gathered. Under the porch light, Sonny's brother-in-law spoke up.

"Sonny was at a ceremony for Sam. Sam's family had called in some elder medicine people because things were flying off the wall, people were being thrown to the floor, things like that! The medicine people told the family that Sam was angry because of the way he died, so they were holding a ceremony at the body to direct his spirit, let it understand what happened to him, and help it onto its journey."

The brother-in-law continued, "Sonny joined the ceremony, and during it he got sick, real sick. He wanted to leave the circle, but the elders told him not to. He left anyway and came home, and something awful came with him!"

"My God," I said to myself, clutching the cedar and sage. Looking into the darkness, I was having second thoughts about going alone through the woods back to my camp. But I politely turned down a ride and struck off walking. I had nothing to fear, did I?

I had a flashlight with me and it helped, but I couldn't get that picture of Sonny being pounded against his bed out of my mind. I must have been about halfway back to my camp when a horrible smell almost gagged me. I hadn't noticed that smell as I came by here not thirty minutes ago. That's when I noticed it was getting colder. Then I could see my breath. I had chills. Suddenly my flashlight went out. I was panicking, shaking that flashlight and hitting it against my leg until it came back on. I was still a good city block from my camp and I wanted to run, but I knew there was a powerful force with me. Something kept telling me to pray, and I did out loud.

The words "something awful came with him" kept repeating in my mind. On what had been a warm, clear night, the freezing air bit at my skin. My light kept going out. And that god-awful smell . . . I was scared. Only a few yards from my tepee a wind slammed into me, making me fight the last few steps to the door, then whipping the door into the air like it was trapped in a whirlwind. I grabbed the door, ducked inside, and desperately tied it down. Inside I stoked hot coals still in the firebox, then sprinkled cedar and sage over the coals. As the smoke rose, I felt a weight lifting from me. My tepee warmed. Outside, I could hear that the windstorm had ceased.

I didn't sleep that night. I just kept the fire going, and now and then I'd burn a little more cedar and sage, until the sun came up at last—to a very beautiful day.

I made my way over to Sonny's house, and there he was, outside, walking with a cane. He looked noticeably older.

"Are you OK?" I asked.

"Yeah, I'm fine." His voice didn't sound the same. "The funeral is today; are you going?"

I looked down. "I don't know if Sam told you about the deer we shot, the day of the accident. We hit it in the same place at the same time. I don't know what it means, if anything, but I do believe things like that happen for a reason. And I do believe it has connected us in some way. So, if you don't mind, I think I'll stay here."

The Rock Baby

TRADITIONAL KAWAIISU TALE, CALIFORNIA

*Have you ever seen a pictograph—ancient artwork that is inscribed
on a rocky cave or cliff? Don't touch it, says a legend of the Kawaiisu
people of California's Sierra Nevada. It belongs to the spirit who
lives inside the rock: "Rock Baby," or "uwani azi." Its name in Kawaiisu
sounds like the cry an infant makes: "uwa uwa." The picture is
always changing, say the Kawaiisu, because Rock Baby
is always working on it. A passerby must never touch the art—
or look upon the artist.*

Some people who lived along the south fork of the Kern River went
out to gather chia seeds. It was a beautiful sunny day. The pop-
pies and clover were blooming along the river, and as the people
walked toward the desert, they began to notice the rock walls were covered with pictures of people painted in red and yellow.

All was quiet as they hunted for food. One man wandered especially
close to the rocks as he gathered his food.

"Uwa! Uwa!" cried a small voice from above him.

The man looked up. There he saw a crying infant wedged between two
rocks. It had no blanket or other covering. Even though the sun was
shining, it appeared to be shivering. He made his way up the hill, gathered the infant into his warm, strong arms, and carried the child gently
down the rocky slope.

"Come and see the child I've found!" said the man.

The people looked at the man as he stepped down from the rocks. Quickly they put their hands over their eyes. They were afraid to look.

"It could be Rock Baby!" cried a young girl. "Don't you see that he has been working on his pictures right here?"

"He will harm you!" an old woman gasped.

But the man looked at the baby and felt sorry for it. His wife left her women companions and came over to join her husband. She, too, looked at the baby. The child's small round face cooed up at them. Its head was covered with thick black hair. They could not tell whether the child was a boy or a girl. It continued to coo in sweet, low tones.

"We must take the child with us," said the wife.

The couple had recently given birth to their own baby. They agreed that they should bring this child home as their own. But the others continued to call out to them in fear, their eyes covered.

"Take him back!" cried the young girl again. "He will bring harm upon all of us!"

"Listen to her!" The rest of the party joined her plea. They all turned around and began to run back toward the river.

The baby began to cry now, and the husband took even more pity on it. He cooed back, stroking its hair. But the wife stopped. A chill ran through her. Something in its cry did not sound like the baby's cry she knew so well from her own child. It sounded ancient and evil. The wife became frightened.

"Take the baby back where you found it!" she cried suddenly. "I will wait here. But go quickly. Soon it will be dark and we'll lose the others."

Sadly the man made his way up the rock face. As he climbed, he braced himself against the walls covered with paintings in red and yellow and black. The baby quieted and started to coo again.

The man found the spot where the baby had first cried out and gently placed the baby back into its rocky shelter. Underneath the child he placed his own shirt as a pillow. Then he stepped away to take one last look.

To his surprise, the baby stood up. It nodded at him. The sweet, cooing mouth twisted into an evil sneer. Then it turned around to the cliff wall and stepped inside. Tied to its back was a baby's cradle.

It was the last thing the man saw. He was now blind.

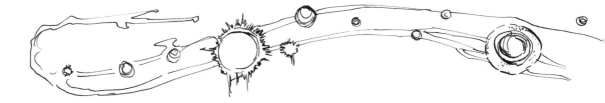

The Little People

TOLD BY DAN SASUWEH JONES, PONCA

In our culture, the Little People are mysterious and often mischievous.
They are said to create colored balls of light that people sometimes see
floating off the ground at night or flying through the air at high speeds.
Little People may use these lights to help them see in the dark, or to
defend themselves. Or the lights may have a power unknown to us.
Where Little People live is a mystery, too. It could be underground,
or in trees. Sometimes they appear to climb out of solid rock or thin air.
At times they can be friendly and at other times harmful. If you make
Little People angry, they may punish you by taking a family member
for a short time—or for a lifetime. In any tribe, it is the elders
who know the Little People best. As a person grows older,
the Little People visit more and more often.

He was ninety-four years old, so I tried to visit him every day, about the same time each day. I thought being on a regular schedule would help him remember me. His memory had been slipping for a year now. He had been telling me some very strange things, but this day his account was exceptionally strange. When he told me stories like this, I would listen intently and do my best to be as understanding as possible.

When I arrived at his home, I let myself into a comfortable environment filled with memories of my childhood. The same photos of family

now grown or passed away covered the walls. There was an unfamiliar smell of old people, musty but not unpleasant. "Hey, Dad, how are you doing today?"

He always answered the same way: "I'm good, and how is the world treating you, young man?"

As he shuffled from the kitchen into the living room, I paused just to look at him. By mainstream culture he is technically my uncle, my father's younger and only brother. But my father had passed away, and in our tribal culture, his brother then becomes my father. Now he was my dad, and I honored him.

"Has your health really been good, Pop? No problems, right?"

He found his favorite chair and slowly got comfortable. "I don't have a whole lot of people coming by these days," he said.

"The problem is you have outlived all your relatives and friends." I smiled, keeping it light. "So what's on your mind, Pop? Is there something I can do for you?"

"I don't know . . . you'll probably think I'm losing my marbles," he said.

"No way," I shot back. "Try me! I'm a pretty easy listener."

"OK, but don't say I didn't warn you, son," he sighed. "I have been seeing those little people our folks talked about all my life."

Now he had my attention.

He continued: "I started seeing them a while ago. At first I'd see them out of the corner of my eye. Or I'd see something move and turn my head, to see it dart out of view."

I nodded.

"And then they began showing themselves. They dart around here all the time now."

Taken aback, I searched for words. "Are they here now? What do they look like?" I asked, looking around the room.

"No, of course not—not when you're here!" he snipped back. "Yep, I had forgotten what the old folks used to say—that the Little People make orbs of light and use them to spy on us. Well, I'm seeing those, too." He looked up at me.

I knew what the old people said. They said other things, too, about the orbs. But he had never mentioned it before, and it worried me. I was concerned that he was lost and struggling for a memory.

"Dad," I said, "I'm calling your doctor to make an appointment. Maybe have him check on your medications. Hey, what if I stay here with you tonight? I'll sleep on the couch here."

He just smiled. "Well, if that's what you want to do, nobody is going to stop you. Maybe your sister can come over for dinner also? Be nice to have you both, and her little bread snappers," he said.

I was glad to see that his sense of humor and love of my nieces and nephews were still doing well.

"OK, I'm going to call sis and run over to my place to pick up my overnight bag—and I'll be back."

Back at Dad's a while later, I opened the door to find him watching *Dragon Ball* on television.

"I see you're up with the latest programs on TV, Pop." I smiled. As I watched, I saw the characters from the show throwing balls of brightly colored light as weapons. I wanted to believe that this was the reason he was talking about orbs of light.

My sister and her kids stopped by. They didn't stay long. Then after dinner Dad and I continued our talk about the old days. At last I could see Dad was tired, and I walked him to his room. I had made up my bed on the couch, and it didn't take me long to drift off.

Sometime in the middle of the night I woke up in what should have been a dark room. Instead, it was glowing blue, from a light coming from under Pop's closed door, all the way down the hallway. I also could hear a humming sound like an air conditioner running. But it was winter!

In three strides I was at his room, opening the door. I gasped. Dozens of ball-like orbs of different colors floated in the air. They were all sizes, but a blue orb was the largest and brightest, its light flooding the entire room. The size of a basketball, the orb hovered right above my father's chest as he lay in bed. Other smaller orbs were everywhere. One passed in front of me and I tried to swat it away, but my hand passed right through it.

As I started easing toward the orb above my father, I had to partially cover my eyes because its glare was so bright. My father, his eyes closed, lay on his back, totally still, as if in a trance. There was no hint that he was aware of the orbs, and there was no sign of pain or distress.

I was in total shock! I didn't know what to think or do. Within seconds, the smaller balls of light began dimming and disappearing. A split second later, the large blue one above my father shot backward like a bolt of lightning, passing through the wall as if it wasn't even there. The room turned dark.

I felt around for the light switch. Strangely, the light blinked a few times before it came on. My father, still lying motionless, wore a tranquil look. But a feeling of fear was sweeping through me. As the different colored orbs crossed my face, bathing the room, the bed, and my father in shimmering light, I was terrified. I knew what the orbs were up to. I shook him to try to wake him, then I felt for a pulse on his wrist. Slowly he opened his eyes. I talked to him calmly, telling him the ambulance was on the way. It seemed like forever, but I finally heard the siren.

At the hospital, my father slept. I don't know if he could hear me, but I told him that the Little People had been with him and that he had not been imagining things.

"I saw the orbs myself, Dad!"

When the doctor came in, I excused myself to the waiting room. My mind was racing through so many things about this evening. The orbs. My father's peaceful face. His words about the Little People.

My sister had arrived, anxious to see him. As we sat there, waiting to go back into his room, it suddenly came to me. I turned to my sister as the words slipped out: "Do you remember what the old people would say about the Little People coming?"

"No, I don't remember anything like that. Why are you asking me that?" My sister was glaring at me, waiting for an answer.

I started to speak as the doctor walked into the room looking sadly at us, shaking his head.

"They'd say the Little People come to take you home."

La Llorona

BASED ON A TRADITIONAL TALE FROM INDIAN TRIBES OF THE SOUTHWEST,
TOLD BY BROCK BATTENFIELD, SMALL TOWN MYTHS

*The spirit La Llorona—the weeping woman—is said to come from an
ancient omen that foretold the ruin of the Aztec people of Mexico and
their ruler, Montezuma. Aztec goddesses predicted that just before
Montezuma's downfall, the voice of a woman would be heard crying in
the night for the fate of her children. In 1521, it came true: Soldiers led
by the Spanish conqueror Hernán Cortés marched into Montezuma's
kingdom and destroyed it. Just before they arrived, Montezuma is said to
have heard "a woman who roams the streets weeping and mourning."
As the centuries passed, Nahuas and other descendants of the Aztecs,
including many Indian tribes across the American Southwest,
have told their own versions of La Llorona. The tales usually involve a
rich Spanish man who marries an Indian woman—then betrays her.*

Maria was a pretty young Nahuan woman who lived in a rural
village in Mexico. Her people were descendants of the ancient
Aztecs. One day, as she went about her usual chores, she was
approached by a wealthy and handsome young Spanish nobleman who
happened to be passing through. The man was so taken by her beauty
and grace that he asked her to marry him.

"Yes," she answered shyly. She was very excited, as was her family.
The nobleman's father, however, was less enthused. By marrying a girl
who was an Indian, he thought that his pure Spanish bloodline would

be spoiled. But the young nobleman was in love, and he would not listen to his father.

The couple built a home in Maria's village. For a few years they lived in happiness, and together they had two young boys.

As time passed, the man traveled more often. Maria and the boys missed him, but they always looked forward to his return and their time together as a family.

Then, one day, he returned home with a younger woman. He said good-bye to his sons, and he told Maria that he was leaving her to take the woman as his new wife. She was wealthy and had been born to nobility. They would live far away, on his father's estate.

As her husband and his new bride rode off, Maria became furious. She grabbed the two boys by the hand and pulled them to the nearby river, the Rio Grande. Enraged, she drowned her children in the fast-flowing waters. As if in a trance she watched them float away. After the two were gone, she realized what she had done.

"My children!" she screamed. She frantically searched the rapids for her sons, but could not find them.

Days later, Maria was seen, delirious, on the riverbank. Her clothes were wet and slick with mud. When a passerby tried to help her, she clawed at him, then ran away, screaming, searching like a madwoman through the tall grasses on the riverbank.

Legend says that Maria had drowned herself, but she was stopped at the gates of heaven. There, she was questioned about the location of her children. When she didn't have an answer, she was sent back to find them. Now she is cursed to walk the Earth as a tormented soul, searching for her sons. With screams and wails and cries, she will stop travelers along the river road, asking where her children are.

The local people have named her La Llorona—the Weeping Woman.

One South Texas man claims that while making his regular drive home one night, he met La Llorona. The road was black and deserted beneath the dim, faraway light of the stars. He could see nothing but what was in his headlights, not even the river beside him. Then he came across something he had never before witnessed on the road.

A woman with long black hair and a white dress was walking along the shoulder. As he pulled up slowly behind her, he noticed that she was soaking wet. Concerned, the man rolled down his window and called out, trying to get the woman's attention. Unluckily for him, he succeeded.

Slowly, in the headlights, the woman turned to him. She was pale and very thin, and her flesh appeared to be decaying, almost falling off her bones. She was crying loudly.

The man was still worried for her—until he looked her directly in the eyes. The sockets were empty—nothing but solid black holes.

"My babies!" She opened her mouth wide and let out an earsplitting scream.

Racing toward the car, the emaciated woman extended her bony arms and reached for the handle on the passenger door. The man floored his gas pedal, spinning his tires to get distance from the monstrous creature.

When he looked back in the rearview mirror, she had vanished.

CHAPTER THREE

Witches

A witch is a type of medicine man or woman—usually one who goes to the dark side. Witches can do terrible things, such as putting curses on people. In the worst cases, they use the human emotions of hate, greed, anger, jealousy, or revenge to help a person get even with someone who has wronged them. But witches can also do good things. They can find things that have been stolen or lost—or even a loved one. They can also help a person regain self-respect or another's affection. A witch must always be paid twice. Once when their service is requested—as a small offering, such as a blanket or some money. At that time you tell the witch what was taken from you or done to you. The witch will then determine what he or she is prepared to do for you. Later, you are expected to pay up when the witch determines the agreement has been fulfilled. If the witch finds out that your complaint was actually your fault, the witch may come after you! What can witches do to you? They can make you or your family sick. They can burn down your home without setting foot in it. They can even send an evil doll to kill you.

The Walking Doll

TOLD BY DAN SASUWEH JONES, PONCA,
VISITING THE WARM SPRINGS CONFEDERATED TRIBES, OREGON

Languages, ceremonies, and governments can differ greatly from tribe to tribe and region to region. This tale took place on the Warm Springs Reservation, in Oregon, where three tribes—Warm Springs, Wasco, and Paiute—live close to one another but have different traditions. Supernatural spirits are different, too. Ghosts, monsters, and witches have different roles in different cultures. That includes the role of the walking doll witch. Depending on the culture, a medicine person may fashion such a doll out of deer antlers, or cloth, or perhaps leather. Maybe it is carved from wood. Whatever their origin is, all walking dolls have one thing in common. Each one is inhabited by an evil spirit, and each one "walks" to deliver its frightening message.

Cody was driving home from work along the same river that his wife's family had owned for generations as members of the Warm Springs tribe in Oregon. Ahead of him a construction crew was uprooting some large old cottonwood trees. As he looked at the large root ball of one big old cottonwood, it appeared to have three distinct root balls, as if three young trees had grown together to create a massive old tree.

Those trees have been in this earth a long time, Cody thought. *What a shame they can't be used for something.*

The flagman waved him through, and Cody drove the short distance home without another thought.

Later that night, at his home with his family, he heard a *thump, thump* on the front door. His two dogs started barking. It was way too late for guests, especially because they lived far from the tribal community.

Cody turned on the porch light and peered out the peephole. He didn't see anyone there at all.

That's strange, he thought as he opened the door. No one was there. He walked to the edge of his porch and peered into the darkness. Nothing. He walked across the porch. Nothing. Then the porch light flickered and went out. He stood there a moment, his eyes adjusting to the darkness.

Something streaked across his porch from one side to the other.

In the darkness, he immediately thought it was an animal. But it was too big to be a mouse. Too fast to be a skunk or raccoon. Too close to the house to be a bear. He shook his head, stepped inside, and closed the door.

Then a scream came from his daughter's bedroom. "Dad, something was trying to open my window!"

"OK, that's it," Cody shouted. "We have an intruder!" From the hall closet he grabbed his shotgun and flashlight and made his way back outside, with the dogs.

Cody stood on the porch a few minutes and listened to the night. It was strangely quiet—no frogs from the river or the other usual sounds. Suddenly, the dogs pulled away and ran into the darkness. Moving cautiously around his house, he shone his light into his smoke shack, where the family smoked salmon, then moved down by the river and along a short trail to the family's sweat lodge and other outbuildings. Nothing. After circling his property, he returned to his front porch.

That's when something tore through the tall grass, chased by the dogs barking at the top of their lungs. *Swoosh* went the grass as something small sped through it. What was it? He either had to force it out of the grass or run it off.

Then a dark streak broke out of the tall grass and aimed right toward him.

He raised his shotgun, but it was too late. The thing had clawed through his pant leg and now latched on to his boot, snarling. Cody couldn't shoot it for fear of shooting his own foot. He kicked. He swatted. At last he used the barrel of the shotgun as a club to knock the thing away. But it wasn't letting go.

What was it? All he could see of the vicious little thing was a snarling, shaking ball of hair, just a little larger than his foot.

Within seconds one of his dogs snatched the creature off his boot and violently shook it so its hair flew in every direction. Free of the thing, Cody still couldn't shoot it because his dog had it. Suddenly the dog yelped as the thing lashed out and got away.

Cody had dropped his flashlight, but by the moon he saw the thing run into a crawl space under his house. Soon the dogs were barking into the space's black entrance.

Frantically, Cody walked in circles, looking for his flashlight. He found it and raced to join the barking dogs.

He scanned the crawl space—past floor beams, pipes, and brick supports for the floor, all hiding spaces for whatever was under there. Then, to get a better look, Cody scooted halfway into the crawl space, shotgun first.

There it was—its back toward him—a ball of fur. Then it slowly turned around. Cody saw that its decayed face had no eyes. Only its snarling mouth filled with sharp teeth glinted like diamonds in the light from his flashlight.

"What are you?" screamed Cody.

The vicious thing flew at him.

BOOM! In a split second Cody took aim and shot. The blast in the confined space was deafening. What he saw was even more shocking. The hideous thing had exploded. But instead of blood and bones, it left a pile of black hair and pulverized stuffing of white cattail fibers. Cody lay exhausted.

"Cody! What is going on!" His wife startled him, shaking his legs where they stuck out of the crawl space.

"Call the tribal police—right now!" he cried. Then he lay in that entrance for half an hour until the police arrived. If he took his eyes off the creature's remains, he feared it might come back to life. He did not dare crawl under to retrieve it.

After the police gathered the remains, they dumped them on the hood of the squad car.

"Stuffing, hair, and cedar wood," said the officer, shaking his head as he sifted through it. "Is this some kind of joke, Cody?"

"No, sir!" Cody held out his shredded pant leg. "I didn't do this to myself!"

The officer went on: "Looks like it was a cedar-and-fur doll. The stuffing looks like cattail fibers, something the old-timers used to stuff their quilts and pillows with—also their dolls."

The officer held up a sharp triangular piece mixed into the mess of stuffing. It appeared to be a sharpened shell—and there were several. Then he spoke.

"This is a doll—or it once was. You don't need cops, Cody. You need a medicine man."

A couple of days later, Cody entered the medicine man's home. He placed the remains, now securely wrapped in cloth and tied with a leather lace into a bundle, on the table. Sitting around it were several elders, all holding canes ornately carved with symbols unique to their clans and families. One by one the elders spoke in their native tongue. They never opened the bundle. Most appeared to not even look at it. Then they asked Cody to leave the room while they disarmed the powers of the doll.

When they called Cody back in, the elder at the head of the table spoke, now in English. He told Cody he and his family were safe.

"This being was not intended for or against you." He looked gravely at Cody. "It was created over a hundred years ago for someone else."

"However"—the elder began to unwrap the bundle—"somehow this being has survived, most likely because its reason for being created was never completed."

Cody's eyes were wide as he listened.

Then the elder's voice lowered. "We know the story of this one. It was sent by a medicine man to kill your wife's great-grandfather. But her great-grandfather was a powerful medicine man. He understood evil spirits, and he captured the doll before it did him any harm. Then, because these spirits cannot be killed, he had to contain it inside a living thing."

"What kind of living thing?" asked Cody.

"First, he placed the doll into a deep sleep and tied it up. Next, he wrapped three young cottonwood trees around it, tied them tightly together, and buried the bundle. As the trees grew up around the doll, they contained it."

Slowly the elder finished unwrapping Cody's bundle. There the thing lay. Cody gasped. It had completely restored itself.

It was hideous, a horrific long face carved in cedar with hair of black fur and eyes made of shiny black shells. Its leather body also was covered in black fur. Bear claws lined its feet, and falcon talons stuck from its arms instead of hands. Most terrifying was its mouthful of sharpened shells.

"The doll should have eventually rotted inside the roots of the cottonwood," said the elder. "Then its life force would have passed into the tree and it could never harm a human again."

In a sickening flash, Cody remembered the bulldozed tree with three roots he saw the evening before.

"Instead," said the elder, "it escaped."

Cody asked frantically, "Is the doll dead now?"

"It was trying to heal itself and come back alive," said the elder. "But we have put it to sleep for now and we will contain it—this time for good. See: It's already starting to rot, and it can no longer harm you or your family. You may go home now."

Cody watched as the elders pushed themselves up on their canes and started to leave the table. With a sigh of relief, he took one last look at the partly decayed body, then turned to go.

In that second, its mouth opened.

The Garage Sale

TOLD BY VERNANDRIA LIVINGSTON, NAVAJO, NEW MEXICO

*In the Navajo and many other American Indian tribes, custom holds
that when a person dies, their clothes must not be sold or given away.
They must be burned. Otherwise the person's spirit will continue to live
in the clothes and he or she can never move on to the next life. But what if
a person is still living and their clothes are sold or given away?
That person's spirit still clings to the clothes. If the clothes end up in
the wrong person's hands, they may be used for harm. I was just
five years old when I learned that important lesson.*

My family was having a garage sale at our home in Gallup, New Mexico, on the Navajo Reservation. It was a nice day for spring cleaning, and my parents were selling some of the toys I'd outgrown. My mom and dad were also selling household items and clothes and shoes they didn't want anymore.

A man I had never seen before came to the garage sale and spent a lot of time looking around. He seemed especially interested in my dad's clothes. I watched as, one by one, he piled up the shirts, trousers, and shoes. He seemed very friendly and chatted with my parents. My mom said he was lucky to have found such a bargain. Then he bought all the clothes and left.

I thought this was strange. My dad was a tall, large man, and the man, who could have been from another tribe, was thinner and shorter.

It looked as if the clothes would be too big for him. But maybe he was buying them for someone else. No one thought about it again.

Several days after the sale was over, my dad started having terrible dreams during the night. He could hardly sleep. When the family asked what they were about, he said that the things he saw in the dreams were too scary to tell anyone.

At the same time, other things were going wrong. Our car broke down and appliances in the house stopped working.

Soon sores started breaking out all over my dad's body. They itched constantly. I was scared. My dad went to see the doctor, but after a full checkup and many tests, the doctor couldn't find what was causing the sores. The doctor gave my dad some medicine to soothe the itching, and he went home. But the sores didn't heal.

"Maybe we should go back to the hospital!" I heard my mom say one evening after watching my dad treat his sores.

"No," said my dad quietly, shaking his head. "A doctor can't help me."

Instead of going to the hospital, he went to see a medicine man—a person who is taught to practice traditional medicine and ceremonies. The medicine man told him that his symptoms were not a coincidence. He asked about the man who had bought his clothes.

"Maybe it was someone from the yard sale—from another tribe," my dad said. "Some time ago I had an argument with a person from that tribe—not necessarily the person at the yard sale. But I thought we had settled it and we were all on good terms."

The medicine man asked for the details of the argument and my dad explained it. When he had finished, the medicine man nodded. Then he spoke.

"The person who bought your clothes is probably the one responsible for harming you," he said. "It sounds as if he is still angry with you for something you said, and he used the clothes to practice dark magic—to get even."

The medicine man continued: "He has put something on your land to hurt your family. Now we'll find it and you will get better." Then he prayed over our family to restore the beauty and harmony he saw had been misaligned.

The next day the medicine man came to our house. We followed him and watched from a distance as he walked slowly around to the back door. There he knelt down and pushed away a mound of dirt. From a shallow hole he pulled up a bundle of clothes. They had belonged to my father.

As the medicine man carefully unwrapped the bundle, he found that the clothes were tied around a large stone. The stone was carved with tiny images of our house and car and other family property—and an image of my dad. All the pictures showed some kind of damage or illness. Immediately we understood why we had been going through hard times and why my dad had gotten sick.

The medicine man quietly turned to go, taking the bundle with him. He promised to destroy it.

Little by little, my dad felt better. Soon the sores disappeared, we fixed our house and car, and our family life went back to normal.

But I can't forget. I have remained skeptical of who I can trust—and I learned from the medicine man that it is important to always be kind to other people, no matter who they are.

Besides, you don't know what they're capable of doing.

Exorcism of
the Blood Bull Boy

TOLD BY DAN SASUWEH JONES, PONCA, VISITING THE BLACKFEET TRIBE, MONTANA

*A Wild Spirit in nature is a form of energy that changes the spiritual
and physical behavior of a being, perhaps an animal or human.
Such energy can be good or harmful. Only skilled medicine people know
how to direct a Wild Spirit. Medicine people are a revered kind of witch—
some are very good, and direct a Wild Spirit to heal; some are very bad,
and direct the spirit to be deadly. In the face of a harmful spirit, the
greatest tool a good medicine person can use is love. It carries the
most powerful protection in nature.*

In my travels I found myself staying with a family of medicine people, traditional healers of the Blackfeet people. Old Man, as he was known, was the head of the family—a stunning old soul. He wore black every day—from his black hat down to his black boots—and he was very much respected. He was a traditional doctor who healed people with ancient methods using herbs and spiritual prayer. He knew things about nature and natural medicines that science and psychology have yet to recognize. When you looked into his eyes, you saw a universe.

Old Man and his wife, Agnes, lived on a small farm in the shadow of the far northern Rocky Mountains. Here, Blackfeet lands include

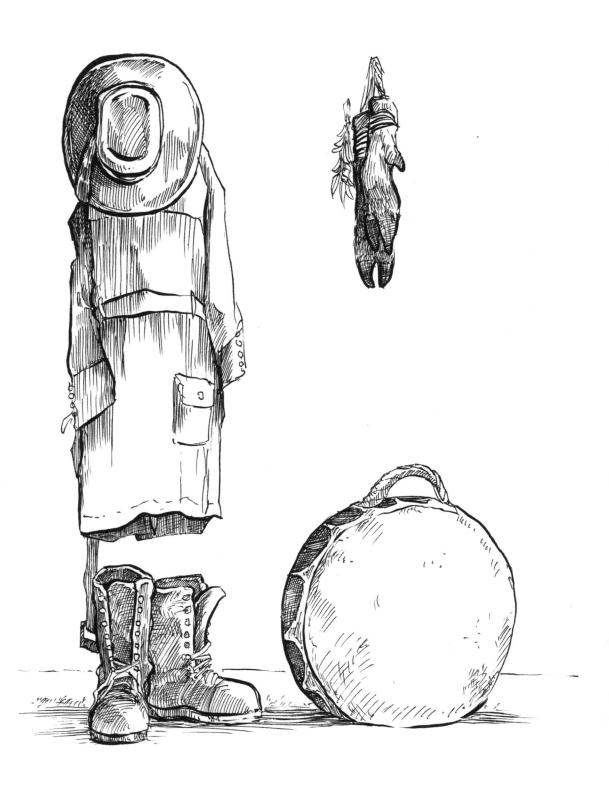

Glacier National Park, called the Crown of the Continent, which includes some of the most breathtaking mountains in the world. The only way in was over a very precarious mountain crossing called Dangerous Trail.

It was Old Man's son, Floyd, who brought me into his family. Everyone called Floyd Tiny Man. Studying under his father, Tiny Man was also an accomplished medicine man.

A whole world revolved around Tiny Man, Old Man, and Agnes. It wasn't just the things we know of in our world. Theirs had another dimension—with spirits, witches, demons, fairies, heroes, and heroines all circling the family's lives. After Tiny Man invited me to stay in the family compound, I became very close to Old Man. Even though he spoke only the Blackfeet language, I entered his world through translations made by Tiny Man.

For three days I had been watching the silver-haired Old Man keep vigil, going outside his cabin an hour before sunset and looking to the north. Always deep in silent prayer, he appeared to be expecting someone or something. What was Old Man waiting for?

On the morning of the fourth day, I was at the corral feeding and brushing the horses and watching Old Man from across the yard. He was in his early nineties, but you wouldn't know it by the way he stood—tall and strong. Judging from his handshake, I'm sure he would beat me in an arm-wrestling contest.

On this clear morning, looking down into the valley, I saw a small red truck racing along the highway. At the entrance to the farm it slowed, then sped toward us up the dirt road, churning dust into clouds. That truck was in a hurry.

I watched as it screeched to a stop in front of the house, and from it unfolded two pretty large Indian men. I later learned they were from the Blood tribe and they had come from Alberta, Canada, to meet Old Man. There had been no phone calls, no letters; they simply showed up. But Old Man had known they were coming. He walked around the house to meet them. As they all conversed in Blackfeet, I watched from a distance, and I realized that *this* was what had been bothering Old Man. But what was "this" all about?

One man went to the back of the truck and pulled out a hindquarter of a very large animal—from its hoof I saw it was a moose. Then he pulled out another. It dawned on me that this was payment for the doctor—people asked Old Man to help heal them by offering food for his family. Things were starting to make sense, but neither of the men looked ill. Then they returned to their truck and left as fast as they had come.

Tiny Man came over to the corral and leaned against the rails. I wanted to blurt out, "What on earth is going on?" Instead, I remarked casually, "Those boys were in a hurry."

"Yeah," said Tiny Man, "they're going to bring their younger brother here—hopefully before sunset."

"Sunset?" I said. It sounded urgent. Whatever Tiny Man was about to tell me would be pretty intense. I bit my lip to stay calm. Tiny Man was nervous—not like him.

After a moment he spoke: "Their little brother has been possessed by a fierce Wild Spirit. The boy insulted a powerful medicine man they call Walking Bear Medicine. He ran away with the medicine man's daughter."

"Do you know this medicine man?" I asked.

Tiny Man nodded, serious. "He's dangerous." As he looked up at me, I could see he meant it. "The brothers told us that when the sun goes down, the boy turns into a bull. It takes four men to handle him because he becomes vicious. They tie him up to control him, but he rages and smashes things. This goes on all night. Come sunrise, he turns back into a human. This will be the fourth night and his family is frantic."

Old Man had agreed to hold a ceremony to help the boy.

Later that afternoon the truck again approached the house. Behind it was a small van. Tiny Man and Old Man appeared on the front porch to greet them. Old Man was serious, but he wore a smile that had the power to brighten any situation—except maybe this one. Things were tense.

The boy's family filed out of the van. Then I noticed the young man—the reason for the visit. He looked like any other young man. Slowly they all disappeared into the house.

Around four o'clock in the afternoon, the young man came out and walked around the yard. I kept my head down as I chopped firewood, not wanting to stare. Then, suddenly, I felt a presence and looked up. I started. He was standing directly in front of me.

"Hey, how are you?" I asked, trying to stay calm. He was just a boy really, yet his very presence chilled me. His eyes, bloodshot from lack of sleep, looked through me with a cold gaze that seemed to focus on something far away. As I took my tools back to the shed, he stood in silence at the chopping block, surrounded by something powerful and frightening that hung in the air. Relieved when one of his brothers took him back inside, I retreated to my lodge for a late coffee. My hands shook as I brought the cup to my lips.

It was getting toward sunset when Tiny Man knocked, and I invited him to have coffee before the ceremony started. No sooner had he sat than a loud thud from the main house shattered the calm. Then another.

Tiny Man shot for the door, and I began to follow. "Don't!" he ordered. "It's started. Stay away!"

Then I heard it. Crashing sounds like people being thrown off the walls. It was all I could do not to run into the house to help protect the old people. But I could not tamper with Old Man's medicine. The crashing continued into the night. From inside my lodge, I could clearly hear Old Man and Agnes praying loudly and singing native songs. The drum seemed to calm the loud snorting and calls that only a bull could make. All night long it sounded like one big fight going on in that small house. I paced around in a circle. What if he escaped? Could I handle him? He was just a boy, wasn't he? Then I thought again: Maybe not.

Gradually the thumping against the walls and crash of objects slowed, then stopped. In the air around the house you could feel that a huge burden had been lifted.

After an hour, Tiny Man came out with the family. The boy still looked like any young man, but something was different. His eyes were clear, his gaze direct, his manner calm.

As the truck and van headed back down the road, Old Man and Agnes stood at the door. They looked tired, but Old Man's smile said that everything was fine. Later, an exhausted Tiny Man came to share the story.

"It was the worst case of a Wild Spirit possession I have ever experienced," he said. "Walking Bear Medicine was so angry with the young man for running away with his daughter that he sent a Wild Spirit of a bull into the boy," explained Tiny Man. "He did it in a clever way, knowing that the young man would listen to the girl he loved. First, Walking Bear Medicine tricked his daughter into telling the young man the story of a boy who had turned into a bull. Then he gave her a charm, carved into the shape of a bull, to pass on to the young man. The young man listened carefully to his love and accepted her gift. Gradually he was so filled with the spirit of the bull that he became one.

"Each night as the sun set the boy's face swelled, his nostrils flared, and his eyes turned into black orbs. He grunted and made deep, inhuman sounds that vibrated in your chest. He flew into a blind rage, and all his brothers and uncles could barely hold him down. He was no longer the boy but the spirit of the bull. Each morning he returned to himself, but his family knew that one day soon he would not come back."

I was silent for a while, taking it in. "How did Old Man get rid of the spirit?" I finally asked.

Tiny Man looked at me knowingly. I could tell this was a secret he couldn't share. "All I can tell you is that Walking Bear's medicine is evil and it represents hate and fear. Old Man's medicine is good. It is filled with love, and in the end, love is stronger than hate."

The Lost Hunters
and the Skudakumooch'

A TRADITIONAL MALISEET TALE,
TOLD BY MRS. SOLOMON, MALISEET, NORTHEASTERN CANADA

*An undead ghost-witch called Skudakumooch' (skuh-deh-guh-mooch)
haunts tales of the Maliseet, Micmac, Passamaquoddy, and Abenaki (the
Wabanaki tribes) of northeastern Canada and the United States.
Skudakumooch' comes alive after an evil shaman—a kind of magician—
dies. The body refuses to stay dead, and it allows a demon to possess it at
night. Then it rises as a ghost-witch to roam the Earth, looking for
human victims. If you are unlucky enough to hear the voice of
Skudakumooch' or look into its eyes, it will cast an evil spell over you.
Then it will kill you and eat you. Skudakumooch' can be destroyed,
but only by burning it to ashes so it can never rise again.*

Two hunters went out hunting. While they were far away from
camp, a big snowstorm blew up, and they got lost.

After hours of wandering in the cold blizzard, they came to a
deserted maple sugar camp. At the center of it was a vacant log hut.

"Let us stop here for the night," they agreed.

But the first hunter said, "I don't feel like going inside that place. It
seems to be haunted by something. I don't feel right going in there."

"Well," replied the second hunter, "we'll have to stop *somewhere* overnight rather than walk in that storm or freeze to death. This might as

well be the place. We can dry out our clothes, and we'll start again first thing in the morning."

So they went inside the creaky old cabin. Cobwebs covered broken furniture, and old bones lay across the floor. The place was dark and cold, but soon they'd built a fire and warmed up. They always carried dried deer meat and moose meat with them for their lunch, so they ate what they had left. By the firelight they saw bunk beds in the corner, and they decided to lie down to sleep.

"What is this?!" The first hunter jumped back as he looked down at his bed.

A dead man was lying in the bottom bunk, on top of a bed of fir boughs.

"I'm not going to sleep here, next to a dead man!" he said.

"Why not?" the second hunter replied. "What harm can a dead man do us? He'll never hurt us. I'm going to stay here rather than walk outside in this storm."

The second hunter soon fell asleep and was snoring.

But the first hunter couldn't sleep. He almost fell asleep once, but he was cold and he got up to put some more wood on the fire. When the crackling of the new wood died down a little, he could hear another noise—a kind of gurgling noise. He looked across the room, then he looked to his sides. Then he looked behind him.

There he saw the dead man sucking the blood out of the neck of the other hunter. The dead man had come to life.

"Skudakumooch'!" the hunter realized in horror.

Now this hunter picked up a bone lying near him on the floor and threw it with all his might behind his left shoulder to ward off the weird creature.

Crack! He heard the bone hit the monster as his fingers fumbled to put on his snowshoes. Then he left the cabin grounds as fast as he could.

As he fled through the woods toward his home, he had to cross a lake covered with ice. He slipped and slid; sometimes his snowshoe crashed through a soft spot in the ice. Every once in a while, he'd look behind him.

Soon he saw a big ball of fire coming after him. He was partly across the lake, but this ball of fire was flying so fast that it was almost catching up with him. He sighed with relief when he reached the other side. But the ball was coming closer. And now he could see his village in the distance.

"Help!" he screamed as he ran, trying to draw the other Indians' attention. When they heard him, they also saw this ball of fire chasing him. So they all took their bows and arrows and shot at the ball of fire. That's the only way they could make it turn back.

Then the hunter fell into their arms. He was unconscious. They carried him home, and after they cared for him and he had come to, he told them the story about the dead man at the maple sugar camp.

The next morning they all went to that place.

Just as the hunter had described, inside the cabin they found the dead man lying on the bunk—right where the hunter had first seen him. On the other bed they found the other hunter, with his jugular vein broken open and the blood drained out of him. Carefully they took him home and buried him in the Indian burying ground.

But the other one?

The dead man they burned. They tied him to a pile of wood and lit it on fire. That's the only way they could kill him so he wouldn't bother any more people. As Skudakumooch' went up in flames, they could hear the bones cracking.

And way off into the air, the fading sound of a screeching voice.

Hand Games:
Tiny Man versus
the Witch Twins

TOLD BY DAN SASUWEH JONES, PONCA, WITH THE BLACKFEET TRIBE, MONTANA,
VISITING THE STONEY TRIBE, ALBERTA, CANADA

*There is a centuries-long history of hand games among and between
tribes across America, Canada, and Mexico. These ancient games include
skill, luck, and something deeper that's hard to describe. Two teams face
each other, making dance-like motions with their arms and hands as
drums beat faster and faster. Each team has a set of bones and a set of
colorful sticks. One captain guesses who on the opposite team is hiding a
bone in each hand. For each wrong guess, the other side wins a stick.
The team that wins all the sticks twice wins the game. Hand games
can bring out the good and bad in people. Sometimes a trickster,
a devil-like character, might help an evil player. The loser could end up
with a deformed face or body . . . or even dead.*

The Stoney people of West Central Alberta, Canada, in the Rocky
Mountain foothills, were hosting a hand games tournament for
tribes across North America. I had traveled with the Blackfeet
from Montana to play.

Hand games were important to our tribe, and to me. A hand game is
more than a game. It can reveal a tribe's strengths and weaknesses or

it can be a ritual for healing. When my aunt became ill as a child, the game was played over her, and she recovered. This tournament would be played for money.

Our Blackfeet captain, Tiny Man, was already famous. From the time he was a young man, he had won some of the largest competitions in North America. Now he was a full-fledged medicine man, and his reputation had increased. He had mathematical skills, he was observant, and he knew all the tips and tricks of the game.

When Tiny Man was going strong, he could play three days straight and take only a few breaks. This was not a game to him: It was his life—and he was serious about it.

At the Stoney tournament there was another team who would have to be taken very seriously. This team had two captains—a rare thing. They represented the Cree Nation, from southern Canada to the Arctic Circle. The captains were twins—a brother and sister. They looked exactly alike. Both were medicine people, and they worked together to heal tribal members. They also played the hand game together, taking turns to make the calls. They often won. You never heard them speak to each other, but they appeared to read each other's minds. They both knew at once where an opposite team was hiding the bones, as if they were seeing through your hands. They both looked at their opposing players with cold black eyes.

Tiny Man knew that when we faced them, our two teams would have an amazing game of skill and magic.

Teams usually play over a three-day period. Gradually, the losing teams are eliminated. On the first day we won all our games. By the third day, our team was still winning most games.

The whole time, I was keeping my eye on the Cree twins' team. They were having a successful tournament, too. For all of us, lack of sleep was beginning to take a toll, and I hoped they would make mistakes.

Early on the third day, we made it to the final match. First, we watched the Cree twins' team play an intense game against the Crow team. Our

Blackfeet team would play the winner to determine the tournament champion. It was an exciting time!

The twin brother was like a sorcerer waving the most important stick—called the kick stick—like a wand. Each time the brother screamed out his calls, everyone in the area froze. Little by little, he and his sister were finding the opposite team's hidden bones. The twins were winning.

My eyes were tired, but I couldn't stop watching them. Suddenly, the sister turned and looked right through me. Her black eyes were piercing and probing. I had to shake my head to break her cold stare, like a spell. A chill raced through me.

Throughout, I had watched the best player on the Crow team fighting against the twins. The twins hadn't found her bones yet, but they were getting close. Then the twin brother let out a bloodcurdling cry that shocked every player.

Immediately he started playing a song I'd never heard before. Slowly pounding his drum—*thum . . . thum . . . thum.* It sounded like prisoners dragging their feet in a death march. Then fifty more drummers joined him.

"That's not fair!" exclaimed Tiny Man. "That's a warrior honor song for the dead—not for a hand game." The slow, deathly beat continued, putting us all in a trance so we could not play well against them.

Suddenly there was a commotion. Someone was being carried out. As the stretcher came closer, I saw it was the girl who had been doing so well against the twins. She lay unconscious. Their screams and deadly music had affected her badly.

Tiny Man just shook his head. Looking back, we saw the twins winning point after point against the remaining Crow team. The music turned louder, then became a roar, faster and faster. In a few turns the twins had won.

Now we would play them. Our leader, Tiny Man, took his place across from the twin brother to determine who would go first. They guessed back and forth for the hidden bone. Then the twin brother guessed wrong! Our team went crazy with excitement. We would start the game, which was an advantage. Together, the twins turned their evil gaze on Tiny Man.

He ignored them. I looked at all the happy faces of our team members. And then, in a sinking moment, I happened to glance over at the sister. Her mouth, like a half-moon, was twisted into a frown. She was glaring right through me with a look so demonic that I was almost paralyzed. Tiny Man saw it and quickly lifted his drum in front of my face to shield me from her spell.

"You're OK." He smiled and nodded at me. From then on, I made it my business to avoid that twin's evil eyes.

Tiny Man started his music. It was upbeat and strong. Our team guessed where all the twins' hidden bones were, and we won all the sticks. The twins' team never had a chance. At last there was only the kick stick left for us to win. If we won it, we would win the entire tournament.

The twins, their cold black eyes ringed in blood red, sat expressionless. As the losing team, they would begin the final game. The brother took the kick stick and held it high for all to see. But instead of pointing it toward the other team as the rules say, he slowly brought it down and handed it to his sister, sitting cross-legged on the ground.

She placed the kick stick in front of her. As if in a trance, she stretched her arms into the air and arched her head backward with her eyes tightly closed. She dug her hands into the ground, filled them with dirt, raised them up, and slowly released the dirt over her face and body.

Then those cold black eyes opened. She was staring directly at me.

I froze. In the blink of an eye she screamed "INSIDE." She guessed right! My heart stopped as my hands seemed to fly open by a force not my own, and I threw the bones to her side.

Her brother smiled at me with an awful grimace, proud of his sister's twisted talents. The game was not yet over, but we had lost our lead.

It was their turn to hide the bones. *Thum . . . thum . . . thum,* their drummers started the death march again—like a weapon in warfare. I knew Tiny Man could gain control and get those bones back to our side. Tiny Man took up the kick stick.

But wait. Something was going terribly wrong. The twins made guess after guess. And they were right! Our hidden bones just kept landing on their side. At last, the kick stick was theirs. We had lost the game and all our money.

We got up to leave.

Then I saw it. It was quick, but there was no mistaking it. A slithering tail, like the tip of a serpent's body, flicked out from under the twin brother's coat. A trickster's tail.

I looked up at Tiny Man in disbelief. He just nodded.

La Lechuza, the Owl-Witch

TOLD BY LUIS WICHO AGUILAR, WESTERN CARRIZO TRIBE, SOUTH TEXAS

Before telling this story, I had to get my mother's permission—we must get permission to tell a tale of such dark powers of nature. That is our way: We still go by our old traditions. My grandmother shared this story with us over thirty years ago—about a local legend that's been around for many generations. To people of the Rio Grande, La Lechuza has long been known as an old woman who turns herself into a huge owl. Some say it's to seek revenge for her child being taken from her. Others say she simply wants to snatch children and waits in the dark until a child wanders away from home. Whether you believe this story or not is up to you. Sometimes we have to open our perception to ancient beliefs because there's a reason they are told through every generation.

My grandmother came from a long line of *curanderas,* or medicine women, of the Peyote people of South Texas. She grew up on the Upper Rio Grande Valley in an area filled with myths and folklore. Many years ago when she was very young, she was out in the monte (woods) collecting herbs and harvesting peyote with her aunt Teresa.

It was a warm South Texas summer evening, but, my grandmother said, something about it seemed different, as if something was watching them or walking near them.

As they gathered the herbs, she and her aunt Teresa strayed off the path, wandering too far into the woods. Soon the shadows lengthened, and before long it grew dark. When they turned around to head toward home, they noticed it had gotten way too quiet. The crickets had stopped chirping, and the nighthawk birds suddenly spooked, flying off into different directions.

Aunt Teresa got very nervous and grabbed my grandmother's small hand, telling her to follow her closely down the path. As she walked, Aunt Teresa pulled dry Texas sage out of a bag and started to crush it in her hands. She said a prayer and then threw the crushed sage in all directions. "What is wrong?" my grandmother asked at last.

Aunt Teresa answered sternly: "La Lechuza—Owl-witch—is nearby. Her eyes are upon us." Suddenly the silence was shattered by a horrible screeching sound from behind a group of large mesquite trees.

"Do not look at any large glowing eyes!" Aunt Teresa ordered my grandmother. "Just focus on the path back to the ranch house." The frightening noise was coming closer, and they started to walk faster. Aunt Teresa kept saying silent prayers as they walked fast on the path.

My grandmother felt a strange, cold wind hit her from behind. Young and frightened, but also curious, she turned her head back to see what was behind her. There, on the path, towered a huge, shadowy figure. She faintly glimpsed its hideous-looking face and large, glowing eyes. Then she felt a penetrating chill and heard a strange whispering voice in her head—in a language she couldn't understand. Aunt Teresa scolded my grandmother, who turned her head back toward the path home.

"Do not look at the Owl-witch!" Aunt Teresa commanded. Then they heard one final screeching sound fading into the distance.

When they reached the ranch house, my grandmother started to feel sick. Her mother—my great-grandmother Severa—asked what had happened. Aunt Teresa told her that they were chased by La Lechuza. Great-Grandmother Severa was startled and scared. She knew La Lechuza had put some kind of curse on my grandmother.

Quickly, the two women put my sick grandmother on the bed. My grandmother was getting very cold chills and a very high fever. She kept hearing that strange whispering in her head, over and over. Aunt Teresa gave her a bad-tasting tea made from different herbs and peyote. It made my grandmother fall asleep within fifteen minutes after drinking it. In her sleep she was having strange nightmares.

As my grandmother slept, the two women prayed over her while rubbing a fresh chicken egg lightly all over her body. They continued the old folk cure as my grandmother's fever gradually lowered.

When my grandmother woke up the next morning, she felt relaxed and calm. Great-Grandmother Severa came into the room and settled down beside her. Then she told my grandmother the entire story about La Lechuza, the Owl-witch. That she is more than a myth. That she was once a woman whose son had been wrongly killed by villagers for a crime he did not commit. She sold her soul to a devil-like being called *a'pal kamlákio*—evil earth god—so she could turn into a monster owl. Now she takes revenge by swooping down to steal other children.

Now my grandmother was marked by La Lechuza. La Lechuza had put a curse on her. She was cured of the fever and chills, but the moment would never be forgotten. La Lechuza's voice would still haunt my grandmother's mind, reminding her of the event and that she was always close by. My grandmother would have to beware of the future—and be cautious in little-known surroundings.

My grandmother told us this story when I was about twelve years old—not to scare us, but to warn us to be on guard when alone in the deep South Texas woods. There are forces out in this world, she would say, that the modern age seems to ignore. After that, I would often watch my grandmother when she thought she was alone, looking out into the night, into a distance only she could see. The look in her eyes frightened me. The belief in La Lechuza is real for our people.

I myself have never seen La Lechuza, but when I am out in the woods of the South Texas river valley, I have felt a strange and sinister presence around me—a dark existence in the wind.

The Deserted Children

Traditional Gros Ventre tale, Montana

*This Gros Ventre legend is well known among Plains Indians, including
the Cheyenne and Arapaho, and has several different versions. This one,
in which the children meet a deadly witch, tells about the lifestyle on
the Great Plains of Montana, where Gros Ventre hunted buffalo and used
the skins to make clothing and tall, cone-shaped tents called tepees.
As the people moved between hunting grounds, they carried their tepees
and other belongings on sleds called travois (truh-VOY). The story
tells about loyalty and family ties, which are central to all tribes.
In every Indian culture, children are loved and honored, so the
beginning of this tale may surprise you.*

There was a camp. One day all the children went off to play. While
they were gone, one man said, "Let us abandon the children. Lift
the ends of your tent poles and travois when you go, so that there
will be no trail." The people then went off.

After a time the children came back to camp and found everything
gone, the fires out, and only ashes left. They began to cry and wander
about. The oldest girl said, "Let us go toward the river."

They found a trail leading across the river and crossed it. Then they
found a tent pole lying on the bank and picked it up.

Suddenly the screeching voice of an old woman broke the forest silence:
"Bring my tent pole here!"

The children carried it toward her and she invited them into her tent.

At night they were tired and the old woman told them all to sleep with their heads toward the fire. Only one little girl, who had a small brother, pretended to sleep, but did not. The old woman watched them carefully. When she thought they all were asleep, she put her foot in the fire until it became red hot. Then she pressed it down on the throat of one of the children and burned through the child's throat. Then she killed the next one and the next one.

Before she came to the girl and her brother, the little girl jumped up, saying, "My grandmother, let me live with you and work for you. I will bring wood and water for you." The old woman nodded.

First, she pointed to the dead bodies and said, "Take these out!"

The little girl, carrying her brother on her back, buried all the other children. Then the old woman sent her to get wood. Five times the girl brought wood, and each time it was the wrong kind of wood. Cottonwood, then willow wood, then birch wood, then cherry, then sagebrush. Each time the old woman said, "That is not the kind of wood I use. Throw it out. Bring another load."

The little girl went again and again. She cried and cried. Then a bird came to her and told her: "Bring her ghost-ropes, for she is a ghost."

Then the little girl pulled down some of these plants, which grow on willows, and brought them to the old woman. She was glad. "You are my good granddaughter," she said.

Then the old woman sent the little girl to get water. The little girl brought her river water, then rainwater, then spring water, but the old woman always told her, "That is not the kind of water I use. Spill it! Bring another load." Then the bird told the little girl, "Bring her foul, stagnant water, which is muddy and full of worms. That is the only kind she drinks." The little girl got the water, and when she brought it, the old woman was glad.

Then the girl's brother said that he needed to go outdoors to relieve himself. "Well, then, go with the boy," said the old woman to the girl, "but let half of your robe remain inside the tent while you hold him so I know you are still there." Then the girl took her little brother out, leaving half of her robe inside the tent. Outside, she hung the other half of the robe on a metal spike she stuck in the ground. Then she took her little brother and ran.

Seeing the robe still there, the old woman called, "Hurry!" Then the metal spike answered, "My grandmother, my little brother is not yet ready." Again the old woman said, "Now hurry!" Then the spike answered again, "My little brother is not ready." Then the old woman screamed, "Come in now, else I will go outside and kill you." She started to go out, and stepped on the spike. She screamed as blood gushed out of her foot.

Running as fast as they could, the little girl and her brother came to a large river. A water monster with two horns lay there and demanded that they pick the lice off its body. The lice were as big as frogs. The children worked hard; then the water monster said, "Get on top of my head between my horns, close your eyes, and do not open them until we have crossed." When they had climbed on, he dove under the river, quickly swam, and came up on the other side. The children got off and ran on.

The old woman, hobbling behind them, screamed, "I will kill you! You cannot escape me by going to the sky or by entering the ground." When she came to the river, the monster had returned and was lying at the edge of the water. "Pick the lice off me!" it said. The old woman cried, "These dirty lice! I will not!" Then she climbed onto the water monster. "Take me to the other side!" she shouted. He went under the surface of the water, stayed there, drowned her, and ate her.

The children went on.

At last they came to the camp of the people who had deserted them. They came to their parents' tent. "My mother, here is your little son," the girl said, holding the boy out to her.

"I did not know that I had a son," their mother said, turning away.

They went to their father, their uncle, and their grandfather. They all said, "I did not know I had a son," "I did not know I had a nephew," "I did not know I had a grandson."

Then a man said, "Let us tie them face-to-face and hang them in a tree and leave them." Then they tied them together, hung them in a tree, put out all the fires, and left them.

The people had also left behind a small dog with sores all over his body. But the dog had secretly kept a little fire going and had hidden a knife. When they had all gone off, the dog climbed the tree, used the knife to cut the ropes, and freed the children.

The little boy cried and cried. He felt bad about what the people had done.

Then many buffalo came near them. The boy took one look at them and they fell dead. Another look, and their meat was all cut up. One more look and the meat was dried. Then the boy, the girl, and the dog had much to eat, and the dog became well again.

Next, the girl sat down on the pile of buffalo skins and they became smooth like cloth so she could make clothes and tents. She folded them together, sat on them, and there was a tent. Then she found old broken branches and told her brother, "Look at these." When he looked, they became large and straight tent poles. A fine tent soon stood there.

"Go inside and look," she told the boy. He went in and looked. Then the tent was filled with beautiful skins and furnishings, including a bed for them and a bed for the dog. The dog was really an old man who had been treated badly by the people. Now he was comfortable and he became himself again.

The girl made fine clothes of antelope skins for her brother and herself and the old man. The boy looked into the woods, and there was a corral full of fine horses. The girl called bears from the forest and they came gently, as if they were pet dogs, and the girl ordered them to guard the buffalo meat and the horses. The children lived at this place, the same place where they had been tied up and abandoned. They had much food and much property, and they took good care of the old man.

Then the man who had first abandoned them came and saw their tent and the abundance they had, and he went back and told the people:

"Break camp and move to be with the children, for we are without food." Hard times had come and they were starving, so they broke camp and traveled to the children.

When they arrived, the hungry women went to take meat, but the bears drove them away. The girl and her brother would not come out of the tent. Not even the old man would come out. Then the girl said, "I will go out and find a wife for you, my brother, and for the old man, and a husband for myself."

Then she went out into the camp and selected a girl, a woman, and a young man and told them to come with her. She took them into the tent, and the visitors sat down by each of them. She, her brother, and the old man gifted them fine clothing and married them.

Then the sister told her brother, "Go outside and look at the camp." The boy went out and looked at the people. They all fell dead.

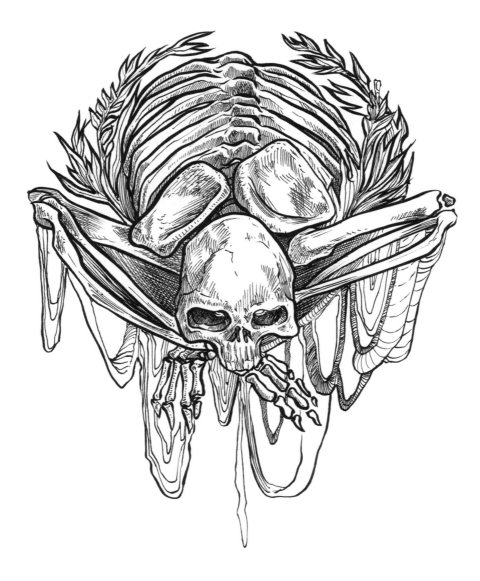

CHAPTER FOUR

Monsters

There are as many monsters in American Indian cultures as our minds can imagine: great and small monsters of every shape and description. Monsters have been part of North American culture since the beginning of time. They are different from tricksters and heroes in American Indian mythology, like Rabbit and Coyote, who help define the identity of the people and their customs. Rabbit and Coyote are sometimes frightening, but they can also be humorous, insightful, and helpful. Monsters, on the other hand, have no redeeming qualities. Some monsters hunt people and eat them. Others terrorize sweet dreams and turn them into nightmares. Still other monsters capture a person's spirit and steal it away forever. Monsters live in darkness just outside our view. If you run into one, your only hope is to outsmart it and escape. Some monsters hide in deep, dark waters where a person must never go. Others make their homes in caves far beneath the Earth. Storytellers may say that monsters exist only in our minds. But then, after a dark night's storm, you may find massive footprints near your home, or the still-warm skin stripped from an animal. You know monsters exist when someone leaves home one night, and never returns.

Pa Ki Sko Kan (Bones)

TOLD BY SOLANGE K., CREE, CANADA

In the northern United States and Canada, winters are long and harsh.
Years ago, food was often scarce in the extreme cold and snow.
Then a starving creature called Wendigo would hunt the countryside
for people to eat. Algonquian tribes describe the monster as "a giant
with a heart of ice," whose body was like a skeleton and whose footprints
were filled with blood. The Ojibwe tell about its glowing eyes and
mouth without lips, filled with yellowed fangs and a long, curling tongue
that unrolls in a loud hiss as it breathes. The Cree tell the legend
of a creature called Pa ki sko kan, meaning "bones."
Do these creatures still exist? You be the judge.

It was late evening, very windy, with snow swirling around—I love this kind of weather. I was about twelve years old and I wanted to play outside. When I asked my mom, she just said, "Be careful."

I put on my boots and winter gear, but as soon as I stepped outside, I had an uneasy feeling. I didn't go out very far, just stayed close to the house, beneath the little roof over the doorway, above the steps.

Then I heard something nearby—something I'd never heard before. I stood still, and was trying to figure out what it was. It sounded as if something was clapping its hands together. Frozen with fear, I listened as the sound came again and again.

Something told me not to go out in the open.

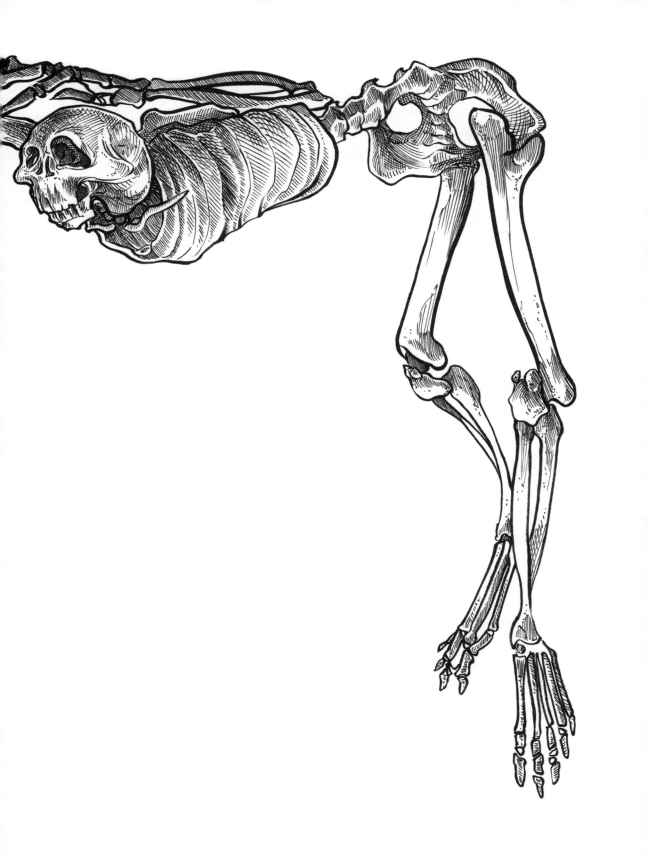

When I looked up to search the sky, I couldn't see anything. Whatever it was, it continued clapping, clapping. It would pause for a moment, then clap again.

You're in danger, my gut was telling me. *Don't go any farther.* At first, I didn't.

But something was drawing me toward it. Then, gradually, I moved to the other side of the porch steps. Slowly, I peeked around the corner of the house.

And there it was. Pure evil. Staring at me. Its glowing orange eyes bored into mine. Something massive and gray—I couldn't see if it was a body or a big, detached head—was floating sideways, seven or eight feet off the ground.

A shock, like electricity, ran through my body. I jumped, pulled open the screen door, and ran in, tripping over my siblings' winter boots.

"What?" my mom cried out. "What's wrong?" She looked up from the stove, where she was cooking dinner. She was bewildered at my panicked face.

"I tripped on the shoes," I said, unsure how to explain it. She let it go.

Years later, I told her. She listened intently, nodding her head.

"I wondered about that night," she said. "There is something that folks have always talked about—a thing that flies around on windy days and during blizzards. It is silent, but it takes people, and no one sees those people again."

She called it "Pa ki sko kan," meaning "bones." It's a legend of the Cree people, and they say it does exist. One of my uncles saw it, and he hid from it when he was out hunting. But that's his story, and I believed him.

When I think back now that I'm older, it made a sound like the flapping of wings—and we don't have big birds in my territory.

To this day I get uneasy when I'm outside in weather that's really windy—even though I live in the city now. I still remember that moment as if it happened yesterday.

If I had stepped out, I don't think I'd be around.

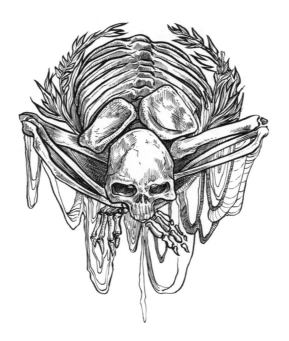

Billy Goat and Bigfoot

Told by Dan SaSuWeh Jones, Ponca,
visiting the Colville Confederated Tribes, Washington State

*On an Indian reservation the people are bonded by a common language,
customs, the land, and a government that is unique to that place.
They are also bonded by beliefs and legends. The bands of the Colville
Confederated Tribes tell of a giant, hairy being with a nauseating stench
who walked their mountains and woods. One band called him Choanito,
the Night Person, another Skanicum, or Stick Indian. Many know
him as Sasquatch, or Bigfoot. Today many people leave the reservation
for the city, but many stay and carry on the tribal stories and traditions
of their ancestors. Billy Goat had chosen to stay.*

My travels had brought me to North Central Washington State, a few miles from the Canadian border, to the Colville tribal lands, some of the most remote lands in America. I was living in a cabin on the banks of the Columbia River. An elder gentleman who everyone just called Billy Goat had rented it to me. The cabin had running water (but an outside toilet), a woodstove for heating, and a wood-burning cookstove that made anything cooked on it taste so good. Billy Goat was my closest neighbor, about a half mile away. The area around my cabin was wooded and beautiful, but it had one oddity—a creature the locals called Bigfoot.

I enjoyed going out and cutting wood as a break from writing. One day

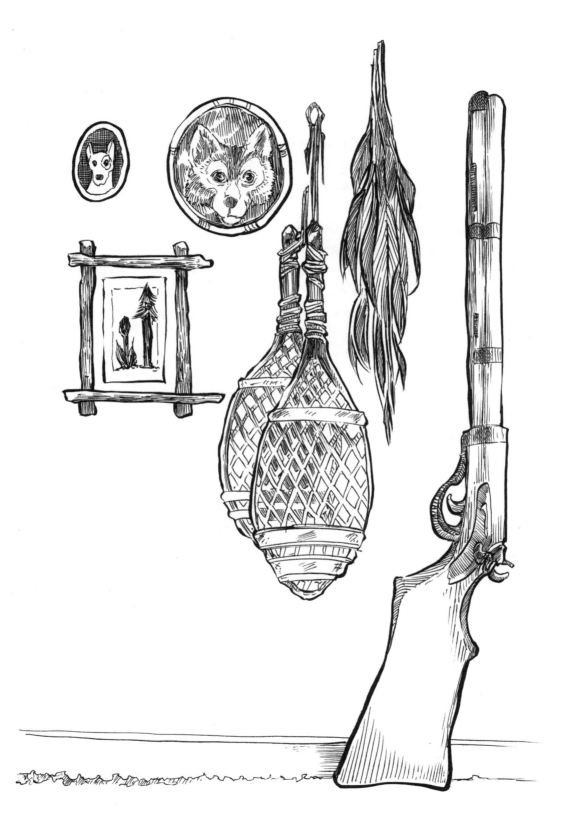

during winter, the fresh snow was about knee-deep. It was a perfect day to bring my neighbor some warmth in the form of firewood, so I loaded my truck. When I pulled up to his cabin, Billy Goat was outside shoveling the new snow from trails he had made to his firewood and outhouse. He always greeted me with a hearty wave and a big smile. Billy Goat was a tribal elder, and tribal members would bring the elder whatever he needed. He didn't even need the wood; I just wanted an excuse to visit him. "Well, hello!" he called out as I parked.

After we unloaded and stacked the wood, Billy Goat invited me into his cabin for coffee. When I entered, it took a few minutes for my eyes to adjust from the bright outdoors. It was like a little museum, with American Indian photos and artifacts either hanging on the walls or carefully placed about his living room. Every time I visited I'd pick one item and Billy Goat would always have a story about it. As Billy was getting the coffee, I was fixated on an old pair of snowshoes hanging on the walls; they were long trail shoes and I could tell they were masterfully handmade.

"What's the story on these classic snowshoes here, Billy?"

"Oh, those, yeah, I made those back in the sixties," he said.

I was taken aback by the craftsmanship to begin with, but now, knowing he had made them, I was in total awe. He brought in the coffee, handed me the cup, and stood next to me as we both admired his handiwork. "My father taught me how to make those, and his father taught him. Last time I wore them, I was tracking a monster."

"Can't get around these parts without them, I guess, unless you have some real big feet!" I laughed, but I was puzzled by what he'd said about the monster. Turning to Billy for an answer, I could see he was deep in thought.

"It started with the fish shack, out back where I smoke my fish," he said out of nowhere. "One night, just last year, I woke to a heck of a commotion, sounded like the fish shack was being torn apart. I immediately thought a bear was in the shack and frightened by the dogs, so it tore its way out. I was sleepy and groggy but it hit me pretty quickly that it was December and bears wouldn't be out—they were hibernating."

He continued, "The other problem was the dogs. They were upset, all right, and barking their heads off, but they were on the porch. That struck me as unusual; when there is a threat they always run after whatever it is. But this time they were trying to get into the cabin.

"When I let them in, I had a pretty good idea what it was—because of the smell.

"Next morning I noticed prints coming up to the shack, then leaving. It was no bear. The tracks were humanlike but much, much larger. Half the shack was torn off and tossed over on the trail like it was nothing. I measured the tracks: eighteen inches long and eight inches wide at the ball of the foot. That was a monster. I followed the tracks into the woods with those snowshoes until I saw them meet up with smaller tracks. Was there a clan of them?"

I was stunned by how the old man's tone was so matter-of-fact, as if he were talking about a normal occurrence. I started asking questions: "So these are the legendary Bigfoot? Are they common in this area?" Now I was thinking of my place just down the road.

"Oh yes," the old man said.

Billy Goat looked out his window, then to me. "Over the years there seems to be a pattern to when they come around. I've never had problems with them until last year."

He turned back to the window as if he were looking far off, back in time. "First it was the fish shack attack, then the dogs. I had three dogs, mainly strays I had taken in, but they had become family. One night I was sleeping when the dogs started barking outside and woke me up. I grabbed my shotgun and opened the door. They'd been cowering and whining, and they were running over each other to get inside. As I turned to ask them what was wrong, a cold chill ran up my back. I turned around to look out, and there was nothing. That's when I smelled him—it stank real bad. I shut and locked the door! I could feel that this new beast was mean and vicious, and the dogs knew it, too!

"The next night things got dangerous. I went to bed the usual time, only to awaken in the night by the dogs going crazy outside the door. They weren't just barking and growling—they were in a fight for their lives. I couldn't grab my rifle fast enough. Then a loud thump hit the cabin and this old place shook. I opened the door and two dogs ran inside. When I got outside, I heard tree limbs breaking as something traveled away fast, from the cabin and into the woods.

"What I will never forget is hearing the third dog yelping for its life as whatever carried it faded into the darkness. When the yelping stopped, I knew it would be useless to follow. Back inside, I sat up all night with the other two dogs, who were traumatized. These things had come before, but never like that."

Billy Goat shook his head.

"At sunrise," he continued, "I strapped on these snowshoes and stepped outdoors to find my dog. I left the others shut in the cabin. It didn't take long until I found the largest footprints I had ever seen. This monster had come right up to my fireplace, where I could see the struggle had taken place—right where I heard the loud thud that shook the cabin. That monster must have thrown the dog against the outside wall and stunned it. I can't believe I was just a few feet away, inside. The struggle lasted maybe five seconds. I could see where the beast had then leaped fifteen feet from the cabin into the woods. By the time I had stepped outside, he was moving away through the trees, breaking limbs and somehow holding a big, struggling dog. He must have been able to see in the dark, because it was pitch-black that night.

"Now, as I followed his tracks, I saw that each footfall was about eight feet apart. That meant he had been moving fast. In my mind I could still hear my dog crying, yelping. I continued into the woods, clutching my shotgun.

"Then I found what would break my heart and send a cold chill through me to this day. Hanging in a tree limb was a long strip of blood-soaked hairy skin—a strip of my dog's hide—no mistaking the color of his hair. That beast was skinning my dog while he was running away with it—like peeling an orange! I tried to remember how long I heard the dog that night. Had that thing killed my dog quick, or was he skinning him alive? My head was spinning. I had seen enough. I turned and headed back to the cabin."

By the time Billy Goat finished his story, I had chills. Now I saw this old man in a new way: It must take great personal strength to still live here, knowing that such a creature could be out there.

I broke the silence. "Where are your other dogs now?"

Billy Goat took a long sip of coffee. "I don't know. After that I kept them in the cabin at night, but over time all I can think is that during the day when the dogs were out, the creature must have gotten them. One by one they disappeared."

"So you think this thing might still be around here?" I said.

Billy Goat looked me straight in the eyes. "I know it is."

The Great Horned Serpent

TRADITIONAL MISSISSIPPIAN MOUND BUILDERS TALE,
TOLD BY DAN SASUWEH JONES, PONCA

*Few stories date as far back in time as this one. Or are as chilling.
This tale may first have been told by the "Old Ones," known to many as the
Mississippian Mound Builders. These ancient people built an empire from
the Great Lakes to the Gulf of Mexico. They left behind massive dirt
mounds, likely used in ceremonies. Today, many tribes believe the
Old Ones are our common ancestors. This would explain why tribes
many miles apart share similar languages, arts, and stories.
One story is of the great serpent called Champie by northeastern tribes,
and Bozho or Man-i-too by others.*

A long time ago a group of five boys were playing on the banks of a great lake. Here, a river poured into the lake. It was a beautiful spot. The powerful muddy river that flowed into the lake formed giant whirlpools as it pressed against the calm blue lake water.

According to the boys' people, you were not supposed to swim here. "It is taboo," the elders had told the boys ever since they were old enough to understand. Now they were twelve years old.

107

Why was it taboo? It was a mystery to the boys.

What the boys did not know as they played along the bank was that the giant whirlpools extended deep down into the water with enough force to drag a whole floating tree to the bottom. No one had the power to swim out of such a whirlpool—especially not a twelve-year-old boy! But there was another secret. Right under their feet were underwater caves, stretching far back into the mountain, carved by the powerful river over thousands of years. And something lived there.

These five boys weren't just any boys. They thought they were the smartest boys in the tribe.

The boys knew that because the place was taboo, no one ever went there. That meant the waters would most certainly have lots of fish—and those fish would be big!

They said to one another proudly: "Who but us would figure out that this spot must have the best fishing around?"

So, one afternoon the boys slipped away to fish at the spot. They didn't bring any fishing gear, no lines and hook, no nets or traps. They didn't want to arouse suspicion back in the village.

What the boys intended to do was to catch the fish by the old style, with their hands. One or two boys would hold a boy by his legs and lower him into the water. There he could feel for fish hidden in crevices along the rock shelf.

But once the boys arrived at the place, they realized the rock ledge was too high above the river for the boys to lower another boy down by his legs. One of the boys, called Possum, had a bright idea. They'd cut a vine from the trees and tie it around a boy's waist. Then the other boys could lower him down.

First they had to find the best place to lower a boy into the water. As they walked along the rocks, they found a long tree branch and used it to probe the depth of the water. To test the current, they threw sticks into the water and watched them disappear as the powerful water dragged them under. As they walked, the muddy river met the lake, and suddenly the water was crystal clear, and so deep they could not see the bottom. They saw something else, too.

A massive underwater cave appeared to extend forever, back into the mountain. It was filled with the fresh, clear water. Possum, being especially smart, said, "An underground spring is coming out of the mountain and flowing fresh water into the river!"

All the boys knew at once: This was where the fish would be. Big fish!

Now, who would go under the water to catch the fish? Possum spoke up: "I will! But first take that vine over to that tree and soften it up." He was in charge, and two of the other boys acted quickly. They seesawed the long vine around a tree until it was limp, but still strong. Now they could tie it around Possum's waist.

"This will work!" he cried. "I won't jump in, but I'll climb down and hang on to the rocks so I can pull myself along the wall above the water and go deep into this cave. That's where the big fish will be!"

Possum lowered himself down the rock until his feet and legs could feel the strong current pulling them outward. He felt around for cracks in the rock he could grab with his hands, and he pulled himself into the cave entrance. Then he ducked his head underwater upside down so he could peer inside.

A beam of sunlight struck the clear water, and Possum saw that the cave was enormous. It sent a shudder through him as he hovered there. As far back as he could see, the cave twisted deep into the mountain—into another world. He completely forgot about fishing.

That's when he saw it.

Something moved. Deep inside the cave. Still submerged, he was running out of air, but he had to see what it was. He grasped the rock, fighting to hold his breath. Straining, he peered far back, where it was dark. One of the large rocks seemed to be moving toward him.

Then there it was. A flash of light glinting upward as a shimmering pattern slid along the rock face beneath him and into a side cave.

In a flash he scrambled upward and burst to the surface, gasping for air. Hand over hand he grasped chinks in the rock to pull himself side-ways along the wall, away from the cave and toward the other boys.

"Pull me up! Pull me up!" he screamed, sputtering as he clung to the rock ledge, his head barely above water, his grip slipping. The current was pulling his legs and body outward.

The boys looked over the rocky ledge and saw the fright in Possum's face. Frantically they pulled on the vine to bring him up, but they had let it out so much that it was long and loose. Pulling it taut took forever. "Pull me up!" Possum screamed again, gripping the vine with both hands.

Then he felt it. A rush of water against his legs. He turned to look behind him, and not six feet away, a massive head emerged. The boys on top could not see it. But Possum did: the head of a giant serpent, five times the size of a horse's head, its huge eyes, narrow slits like a serpent's, focused on him. On its head two long horns swept backward.

Suddenly the boys gave a hard tug on the vine and it jolted Possum upward, onto the rock shelf.

"Don't look!" cried Possum.

But they were curious. Two of the boys peered over the side. The monster peered upward, a sinister smile curling its lips. The boys stared back.

Then, just as suddenly as it appeared, the serpent slid down and away, through the river's turbulent, muddy waters toward the clear bubble of water in the cave. Its long, shimmering body disappeared inside.

The boys stumbled over one another as they ran from that spot. They ran and ran. When they finally stopped, gasping for breath, Possum grabbed each one by the shoulder and ordered him, sternly, "You can't tell anyone, not anyone! They will punish us if they know we were down there in that thing's cave! Promise me!"

And they all did.

The boys went home and didn't talk about the serpent, even among themselves, for many years.

But of course the story did come out, and it's been told for generations. To this day no one goes near that place where the muddy river meets the great lake with its secret cave. Except, perhaps, for one boy.

When Possum's grandson was twelve years old, he thought he was very smart. And he loved to fish.

Then one day he disappeared.

The Chenoo:
The Cannibal
with an Icy Heart

TRADITIONAL MICMAC AND PASSAMAQUODDY TALE,
MAINE AND NORTHEASTERN CANADA

*The Micmac people of northeastern Canada tell of the feared Chenoo
monster, also called the Giwakwa by the Passamaquoddy tribe of Maine.
This man-eating giant was once a human, perhaps a powerful shaman.
He may have committed a terrible crime, like refusing to share his
food so another person starved—or even eating a person. Possessed by
an evil spirit, his heart became a lump of ice shaped like a little human
with perfect hands, feet, and head. The Chenoo prowls snowy forests
eating any living thing it can find with its enormous fangs.
It is always starving and even eats away its own lips. Humans beware:
If a Chenoo does not eat you, its scream can kill you.
The only way to conquer it is to melt its heart.*

A man, his wife, and their little boy left their village in the south
and went north to hunt for the winter. When they found a good
spot, they built a wigwam. The man brought home deer and
bear, the woman prepared the meat, and the boy played outside, chasing after birds and squirrels. Life was good.

One afternoon when the man was away hunting and his wife was

112

gathering wood, she heard rustling in the bushes, as though some beast were brushing through them. Looking up, she saw with horror that it was something worse than the worst she had feared.

An awful face glared at her—an ancient man with wolflike eyes, some combination of devil, man, and beast in their most frightening forms. He rose up above her and bared his teeth, and she saw that his shoulders and lips were gnawed away. She gasped. He had eaten his own flesh. His clothes were rags hanging from his body.

The woman had heard of the terrible Chenoo, the being from the far, icy north—a creature who was once a man but had turned into a devil and a cannibal.

"It is one of them," she said to herself, trembling. Then she thought, *He must not see that I am afraid.*

She ran up to him, calling out in joy and surprise: "My dear father! My heart is glad to see you. Where have you been for so long?"

The Chenoo was amazed at such a greeting. He had expected yells of fear and prayers for mercy. In wonder, he let her lead him into the wigwam.

She was a wise and good woman, and she felt pity as she took him in.

"Father, I am sad to see your flesh so raw and your clothes so ragged," she said kindly. "Come! Let me wash you."

The Chenoo sat silently as she cleansed his wounds. Then she brought a suit of her husband's clothes and told him to dress himself. In his new clothes he sat by the side of the wigwam and looked surly and sad, but he kept quiet. It was all so new to him. Nearby, the little boy played.

Throughout the day, the woman took the little boy with her to gather sticks to feed the fire. It was winter and each day the wind grew colder. The Chenoo watched them go.

On their last trip for the day, the Chenoo rose and followed them. The woman was filled with fear.

Now, she thought, *my death is near; now he will kill and devour me and take my child.*

"Give me the ax!" commanded the Chenoo.

She gave it to him, fearing she was handing him the weapon that would end her life. But he began to cut down the trees as easily as if he were snipping off tiny branches. The huge pines fell right and left, making neat stacks of firewood.

She cried out: "My father, that is enough!"

The Chenoo laid down the ax, walked to the wigwam, and sat down, always in grim silence. The woman and her son gathered the wood and fed the fire. They, too, remained silent.

Soon she heard her husband coming home. She ran out to meet him and told him all about the Chenoo's visit.

"Follow me and do exactly as I am doing," she told him. Her husband agreed.

He went inside and spoke kindly. "My father-in-law, where have you been for so long?"

The Chenoo stared in amazement as the husband told him about their family and about all the things that had happened among their people over many years. The monster's fierce face grew gentler as he listened.

That night the family ate their meal. They offered the Chenoo food, but he hardly touched it. Soon he lay down to sleep. The man and his wife kept awake in terror, watching over their own sleeping child.

As the fire burned through the night and the wigwam grew very warm, the Chenoo woke and asked them to shield him from the fire. He was a creature from the land of ice, and he could not endure heat. The couple put up an animal skin to protect him.

For three days he stayed inside the wigwam, sullen and grim. He hardly ate.

Then he seemed to change.

"Have you any animal fat?" he asked the woman.

"We have much," she replied, and gave him all that she had stored away from the deer and bear her husband hunted. It was cooking fat, and she feared he might now use it to prepare them all in a grand supper. But she smiled bravely as she gave it to him.

The Chenoo filled a large kettle full of the fat and put it on the fire. When the fat was melted and scalding hot, he drank it all in a single gulp.

Instantly his face grew pale and he became very sick. The husband and wife watched as he crawled outside and into the forest. There he retched and vomited up all the horrors and abominations of his life on Earth: all the humans he had eaten, his own flesh, and every other creature. The dead things covered the land. The family was appalled in every sense.

When it was all over, he vomited up a piece of ice shaped like a tiny human. It was his cruel heart. Then he lay down. As the Chenoo slept, the husband took the heart and shattered it with his ax into hundreds of shards of ice. These he melted in the fire.

When the Chenoo awoke, he asked for food, and the woman brought it. He ate much. From that time he was kind and good. His ragged face healed. His evil, meanness, and negativity had melted along with his heart and all the dead things that covered the Earth. The family's fear had melted, too.

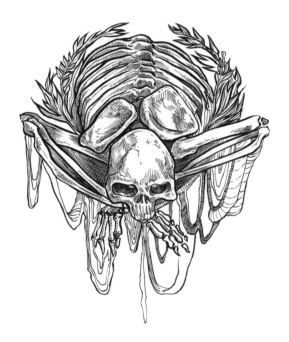

The Vampire of Sleeping Child Hot Springs

A TRADITIONAL NEZ PERCE TALE, MONTANA, TOLD BY ELLEN BAUMLER, FROM *GHOSTS OF THE LAST BEST PLACE*

In 1877, Chief Joseph and his band of Nez Perce Indians were chased by the United States Army over the Lolo Pass in Montana's Bitterroot Mountains. As the small band descended into the Bitterroot Valley, they split into two groups and traveled along two separate routes. One group followed a small creek and discovered a beautiful hot springs. Fearing that soon they'd meet the soldiers in battle, the mothers carefully hid their infants in the thick vegetation along the banks of the spring. Then they moved on with the band, running to escape the soldiers. But the soldiers lost their way in the wilderness, and the battle never happened. Several hours later, the mothers returned to the spring to find their children sleeping peacefully among the grasses, blanketed by the rising fog. They gave the creek and its hot springs the name "Sleeping Child." But there is also another story of the springs . . .

A lone traveler was passing through the Bitterroot Valley. Before him rose the Bitterroot Mountains, touching the sky. Massive ponderosa pines covered their sides like a thick blanket. He had been traveling for many days and would soon arrive home. He thought fondly of his family waiting for him.

Now he followed a sparkling creek that led to a gurgling spring.

"Here is a place to rest and have a drink of water," he said to himself.

Suddenly he heard a sound unlike the usual noises of animals calling to one another along the banks of the creek. It sounded like the pitiful crying of a young child. As he walked closer to the springs, the crying grew louder and louder.

Carefully he parted the bushes along the creek and came upon a child huddled on the bank, weeping uncontrollably.

"Little one," said the traveler, "who could have left you here?" The child was much too young to walk very far, and there were no other villages or travelers in sight.

Lifting the child in his arms, the traveler bounced him on his knee. The child began making sucking noises. The traveler knew that meant the child was starving and wanted to eat. The traveler had just enough food for the rest of the journey, but he would certainly share it with a hungry child. He opened his pack and pulled a little bread from it. He dipped it in the springs to make it soft and tried to put a little in the child's mouth.

But the child would not stop crying. The traveler was afraid he would choke, so to quiet him, the traveler dipped his index finger into the spring and offered it to the child as a pacifier. This worked immediately. The child grew calm, and the traveler breathed a sigh of relief. Then the child began to suck ravenously.

"No!" said the traveler. But when he tried to pull his finger away, he could not. The suction from the child's delicate mouth was too strong.

The greedy child sucked and sucked. Like an enormous suction cup, the child's mouth sucked the flesh from the traveler's finger. The traveler pulled and pulled, trying to extract the bone that was left. The child went on sucking. Soon he had sucked all the flesh from the traveler's arm.

"Let me go!" screamed the traveler.

Before long, the child had sucked away most of the flesh from the traveler's body. As the traveler lost consciousness, his last sight was a great pile of bones from the victims who had come before him.

Soon the child had finished. Full and content, he fell asleep. A few hours later he woke as he heard people laughing and talking in the distance.

The child began to cry.

The Flying Head

Traditional Seneca tale, New York and Ohio,
told by eighteenth-century Seneca chief Cornplanter

*In Seneca legend, the sight of a whirlwind may mean a Flying Head is
near. Also called Whirlwind and Big Head, the Flying Head is an
undead monster that soars through the air, chasing humans to devour.
This massive creature has long, matted hair, fiery red eyes—and no body.
It may be the head of a person who was beheaded, out to seek revenge.
Or it may be a person who was a cannibal then turned into a Flying
Head to chase its human prey. Or it may simply be an evil spirit. Names
such as* Kanontsistóntie's *and* Kunenhrayenhnenh *mean "flying head,"
while names such as* Dagwanoenyent *literally mean "whirlwind."*

There were many evil spirits and terrible monsters that hid in the
mountain caves when the sun shone. But when storms swept the
Earth or when there was darkness in the forest, these monsters
came out to find the people and chase them down.

Among the creatures was a Flying Head, which, when it rested upon
the ground, was higher than the tallest man. It was covered with a thick
coating of hair that shielded it from the sharpest arrows. Its face was
very fearsome and angry, filled with great wrinkles and furrows. Long
black wings came out of its sides, and when it flew through the air, it
made mournful sounds that sent chills through the frightened men and
women. Everyone ran for cover.

The Flying Head was always hungry. On its underside were two long, sharp claws it used to attack its human victims: its favorite weapon.

Before the Flying Head would grab a person, it would lurk around the family's home staking its claim to its next victim. It especially liked to frighten the women and children, mostly widows and orphans. At night it would come and beat its angry wings upon the walls of their houses and scream fearful cries in an unknown tongue. Inside, the little family would close their eyes and hold one another close. When it flew away, the family would breathe a sigh of relief.

But in a few days it would return to snatch and devour one of them.

One night a widow sat alone in her cabin. She had lost all her family—her husband and her small children had been very ill and they had gone away to the long home where a person passes over from this life to the next. Now she was alone. She spent her days hunting in the forest for chestnuts and acorns to eat. At night she would light a fire and roast her little bit of food. Before she went to sleep she would spend hours looking into the fire, dreaming of the happy family life she had once had.

Tonight it was cold. Outside a snowstorm was brewing, and it scooped up snowflakes into whirlwinds around her little house.

The woman built a small fire near the door that warmed her. Into it she dropped a handful of acorns. *Pop! Pop!* The acorns cracked open as they roasted. One at a time she drew them out of the fire and ate them for her evening meal.

She gazed into the coals and dreamed of her little boy and girl running in the sunlight, and of her strong husband returning home through the forest with a deer she would use to make food and clothing.

Swoosh! Swoosh! came a sound outside her home. But the woman paid no attention. She did not see the Flying Head grinning at her from the doorway, for her eyes were on the coals and her thoughts upon the scenes of happiness from her past.

Bang! Bang! Something was throwing itself against her home. At last, the woman looked up, startled. In the open doorway hovered a massive head covered with filthy, matted hair. Its red, glowing eyes bored deep into hers. Its mouth twisted up into an evil grin that revealed sharp, yellowed teeth.

Frozen in fear, the woman had nowhere to run. She watched as its long, deformed claws reached toward her.

The Flying Head floated closer and closer to her, grinning, until she could smell its rotten breath. Slowly it unfolded its claws before her eyes. They reached out, but instead of grasping her, they delved into the fire to snatch her food. It would enjoy an acorn snack before she became the main meal.

Plucking up a clawful of glowing pieces from the fire, it crammed them into its mouth.

AARRR!! Its evil smile turned into a howl of terror. It had accidentally eaten the hottest coals.

AARRRR! It woke the entire village as it escaped into the woods, crashing into trees and rocks as it flew away.

The people were never again troubled by its visits.

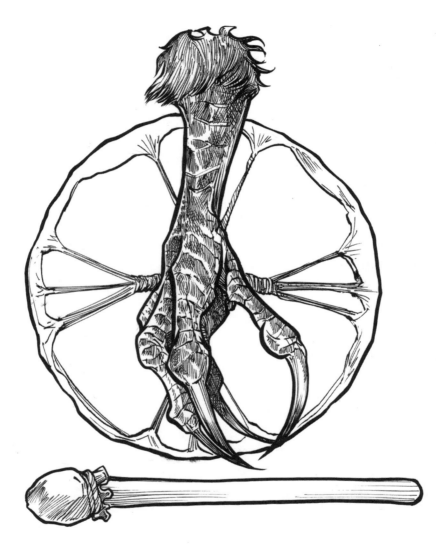

CHAPTER FIVE

The Supernatural

We know we have entered the supernatural realm when strange things that were once only in our nighttime dreams now appear in our waking hours in broad daylight. The supernatural surrounds us all the time. When you walk into a room and a familiar feeling overwhelms you, as if you have done this very thing before, in another time, you are on the threshold of the supernatural. Some people call this feeling *déjà vu,* meaning "already seen" in French. When you enter the supernatural world, you walk through an invisible doorway where the familiar rules of time and space no longer apply. You are in a world beyond the explanation of science and beyond the understanding you have always had of nature itself. The Great Spirit and other good forces dwell here, but so do dark forces. Both forces can shift reality and bring either good dreams or nightmares into a physical form. Through good forces, a mountainous stone may come to the aid of someone in trouble, or loved ones who died may speak to us through animals they once cared for. On the other hand, dark forces may send a monstrous, otter-like creature to prey on unsuspecting hikers. In the world of the supernatural, our imaginations seem to run wild. But what we see is just as real as an encounter in our everyday world.

My Brother,
Last of the Crow Men

TOLD BY DAN SASUWEH JONES, PONCA

My people say there is a spiritual connection between animals and humans. What they mean is humans and animals are the same beings, just in different bodies. Animals laugh and cry just like we do, only in a different way. This story is about a spiritual connection between a person and a crow. Long ago, the Ponca formed a pact with all crows. These special birds were raised by the tribe's warriors and accompanied them when hunting or in battle. The bird-human connection was lifelong, and it followed them into death.

Not long ago, my older brother died.

In our way, we keep constant company with the body for four straight days until the burial. If it's not you who stays with the body, then it's someone else who loved that person. We sit up all night long; sometimes there might be just you, and other times there could be many people. But the body is never left alone. It's common that when anyone has a story to tell about an experience they had with the deceased, that person is free to stand up and speak. Many times everyone will laugh out loud at a funny tale. It breaks the grief, and because you use the same facial muscles to laugh as to cry, it's easy to laugh when you have been crying for so long.

It was the morning of the fourth day, the day of the funeral. We had been with my brother's body through the night, and it was going to be a long day. The small church was full of people that morning—my brother had many friends and family. It was just about daybreak, and I knew my brother's last breakfast would be served soon in a separate dining building just next to the church. We feed everyone who comes, three meals a day for four days. For each meal the body is also served a meal, left on a small stand near the body. It's our tradition. Being the chairman of our tribe at the time, I would be the last one to speak and tell a story about my brother.

I began by reminding my people that long ago the Ponca had formed a pact with the crow. Ponca warriors would raise crows from small birds. The warriors were called crow men—they and their crows were very respected. When a bird was old enough to fly, a warrior would start taking it hunting with him. When the warrior made a kill, whether a goose or deer, the young bird was offered the choicest piece of meat. The liver was always the favorite. This went on for some time.

At first, the bird was always just a guest of the hunter and would ride along on the warrior's shoulder. Sometimes it would fly back and forth from its perch on the shoulder to a high treetop to scout for food. After a season of this, each morning before sunrise as the warrior strung his bow, the bird would be ready to go, seeming to understand what the process was all about.

Over time the bird would change from a guest to a true participant in the hunt. The crow seemed aware that a successful hunt would mean a share in all the meals the prey produced.

Now, with the help of the crow, the hunter could see far and wide. The crow would fly off and find the game, then fly back to the hunter and communicate by special sounds and movements, telling the hunter exactly what he had found. Leaving each morning before sunrise, the hunter and the crow became so in tune with each other that the hunter would know what kind of game the crow had found and even how far away it was. This relationship, this pact between the hunter and the crow, made the Ponca warrior one of the most efficient hunters ever known.

Before sunrise the morning of my brother's funeral, I told the people that I believed my brother was the last Ponca to raise a crow. And I told this story.

My brother Mike raised a crow from a chick. He named him Billy. As Billy got older he went everywhere with my brother, riding on his shoulder. Even when my brother rebuilt an old 1939 Ford truck, then drove it down the dirt roads near our home, the crow would fly along above the truck. My parents would always laugh: They knew my brother was coming home because they could see the crow flying down the road before they saw my brother's truck. Sometimes the crow was ornery and would steal things from around the house. It loved shiny things, and Mom and my sister would have to put away their earrings and other small jewelry to keep them safe.

One day my brother was driving down the dirt road when he had a flat tire. Back then you carried a rubber tire patch kit, with small round rubber patches and glue. He got out his tire tools and opened the kit, but he found he had just one rubber patch remaining. He set everything out on the hood of the truck and began to change the back tire. At that moment Billy dropped out of the air, landed on the hood of the truck, and walked like a person up to the tools and patch kit all laid out on the hood. My brother instantly knew this was trouble!

Mike started to slowly move toward the crow. Billy was looking at the single black patch and then turning to look at one of the tools—a shiny metal scruffer. My brother knew that Billy was trying to figure out which of those things he could carry! Mike hoped he would take the scruffer—after all, it was shiny. Besides, Mike really didn't need it to fix the tire. On the other hand, he needed the patch. If Billy took the last one, Mike would be walking several miles home. My brother eased toward the bird as the bird more frantically looked from the patch to the shiny scruffer.

Should it take the small item or the shiny one? "No, Billy, no . . ." Mike repeated gently. Then the crow, understanding that it was in control of the situation, looked Mike straight in the eye. All of a sudden, the crow reached out and snatched the last patch and leaped into the air. "Billy, stop!" my brother shouted as he ran hopelessly behind and under the crow soaring into the distance. Then Mike walked several miles home.

The churchgoers broke into laughter. It felt good to see all the red eyes laughing. Then, as everyone filed out of the church for the short walk to the dining hall for breakfast, several people came running back in, to grab me by the arms and pull me outside. "You have to see this!" they said.

As I emerged, I saw the trees alive with hundreds of crows, all squawking. Whether they were laughing or crying, I did not know. They covered all the trees, the church, and the surrounding buildings. We had never seen any crows around the church on any other of the four days. It was only that morning, just after sunrise, the same time a warrior and his crow would go to hunt, and just after I had told the story of my brother's crow, Billy. Could these have been the descendants of Billy, come to say goodbye? Not to just one man, my brother, but to the last of the Ponca crow men.

Sleeping Buffalo Rock

BASED ON A TRADITIONAL ASSINIBOINE TALE, MONTANA,
TOLD BY DUCK TO JAMES LONG (FIRST BOY),
FROM THE NATIONAL REGISTER OF HISTORIC PLACES

From ancient times, different stories of the Sleeping Buffalo Rock, which stands in northern Montana, have been handed down among the tribes of today's Montana and Canada: Blackfeet, Assiniboine, Gros Ventre, Chippewa, Cree, Crow, and Northern Cheyenne. Each story tells how the buffalo helped people survive on the plains and how the spirit of the rock gave strength and peace to the people in its shadow. In the twentieth century, a road crew used massive tools to push the rock out of the way, down a hill, to finish building their highway. The next morning the rock was sitting in its original place. Upon consulting a medicine man, the crew was told: "That rock is sacred. It doesn't want to be moved. Let it sit where you found it."

Some years were good for food. Others were bad. One year, game was especially scarce. No buffalo herds came to the area.

The buffalo meant life to the people. They believed that the buffalo held the power of the plains in their large bodies. Not only did the buffalo give the people food and clothing and shelter, but the buffalo spirit protected them.

A few miles from their camp the sacred Buffalo Rock rose above the plains. This ancient rock, in the shape of a massive buffalo, had been here as long as the tribe could remember. The people had heard the

elders' stories. Some said that the place had once been a watering hole where herds of buffalo wallowed, drinking the water and bathing. Gradually, bits of skin, hair, teeth, and bones from thousands of buffalo built up into an enormous rock, covering the hole. The people took comfort in seeing the shape of its horns, hump, and ribs rising into the sky, filled with the spirit of the many buffalo who had come here and formed it. They also knew that the rock was connected to the land beneath it and took great strength from the Earth.

The people also knew that the rock protected and healed. When a baby had been born lifeless, her father prayed to the Buffalo Rock. After many minutes the baby had opened its eyes and screamed its first breath. At other times, tribes at war would meet in the shadow of the Buffalo Rock, intending to draw strength for their battle. But in the end, the buffalo's spirit had calmed them, and they left in peace.

But now, during this time of drought and famine, the people felt that the spirit had abandoned them.

"What can we do?" they said.

"Let us go closer to the Buffalo Rock and pray," they said.

So the people packed up their homes and walked toward the rock. It was a full day's walk. That night they set up camp.

Only one couple lagged behind them. The woman was about to give birth to her first child, and her young husband had been very sick with a disease. They traveled more slowly than the others, stopping often to rest. Each time it was harder for them to get up and keep walking.

"Let us lie down and go to sleep forever," said the woman.

"No," replied her husband. "We cannot give up."

By the time the young couple neared the rock, they could barely walk. They had eaten little bread during their journey, and they were very tired.

The others had already been there for two days. They watched as the young couple approached. They offered to share the little food they had, but the young couple refused to take anything from the hungry people.

They walked past the others, right up to the Buffalo Rock. There they made an offering of their last bits of food. Then they prayed. When they had finished, the young husband and his wife set up their small camp, touching the rock, apart from the warm fires of the other people. While the others slept that night, the couple stayed up and prayed.

The next day the other people said, "We have been here nearly three days and nothing has happened. We have not found any food, and our families are starving. We will have to move on." They began packing up.

"Don't leave," called the young couple. "Let us all pray together. We cannot travel just yet, and if we are all together, we can help each other. If we pray together, the Buffalo Rock will hear us."

But the people packed up and began to leave.

Then the young man looked at his wife, who he loved with all his heart and who was so close to bearing their child. "You must join them and go on without me. Remember me each time you look at our child." Soon he watched her small figure as she trailed behind the others.

Alone, he began to pray again. He prayed that his wife and child would be safe and find food, and that they would prosper. He prayed that death would come swiftly to him.

The tribe had barely made its way to the other side of the Buffalo Rock when a clap of thunder shook the earth. Then another. And another. Quickly the people took shelter under one of the rock ledges. Lightning struck the open ground, and rain hurtled down in sheets.

On the other side of the rock, as the rain poured down, the young man felt his life slipping away. Another clap of thunder shook the air.

Then he heard it. The pounding of hooves. As if the Thunder Bird were pushing some great beast toward him. He opened his eyes in time to see three buffalo racing across the plains before him.

With his last ounce of strength he picked up his bow and arrow, aimed, and shot the buffalo closest to him. With a thump it fell beside him. It looked into his eyes as its life slipped away.

"Thank you," he whispered as his eyes closed forever.

The last thing he heard, in the distance, were prayers of joy.

The Kushtaka

BASED ON A TLINGIT TALE, ALASKA,
TOLD BY BROCK BATTENFIELD, SMALL TOWN MYTHS

*The Tlingit people of Alaska say the Kushtaka are evil spirit beings,
part human and part otter. Their name roughly means "land otter men."
As shape-shifters, they change from one being to the other, and have even
been described as "were-otters." Kushtaka haunt the Alaska Triangle—a
triangular stretch of land from Juneau, the state capital in southern
Alaska, to Barrow, in the north. Across the area's forests, mountains,
caves, and icy landscapes, more than sixteen thousand travelers have
disappeared since 1988. Perhaps fog or freezing temperatures or
avalanches or wild animals are to blame. The Tlingit know better.*

It was Saturday night. A boy's parents were away for the weekend and his friends were hanging out at his house. They passed the time the way high schoolers do, playing video games and watching TV. Soon it was well past midnight, and the boys had gotten bored. Someone suggested taking a nighttime walk through the woods.

They all agreed. The boy's house was just outside Juneau, and it sat near thick woods. The woods were especially scary at night—and the boys were in search of a fright.

The group pulled on their boots, hats, and jackets made for zero-degree weather. They had spent plenty of time in the woods in winter. The snow would be deep and the temperatures cold.

Otherwise, they weren't concerned about anything dangerous. They knew their way through the forest. Because it was winter, the bears were hibernating, and other animals hid when humans came near.

The boys headed out. The night was black, and clouds blocked the moonlight. A faint reflection of light bounced off the deep, white snow. The group could make out only shadows along a dim path into the woods. They crunched the snow as they tramped up a hillside, laughing and joking.

Suddenly someone came running up from the back of the group, breathing hard. Everyone stopped and stared at him.

"You look like you've seen a ghost!" the boys at the front teased.

The boy sputtered: "There . . . there was snow crunching behind me. The steps stayed right behind me, like . . . like it was following us."

"Ha!" laughed one boy. "Maybe it's a Kushtaka!"

The rest of the group fell silent. They began looking behind them.

Since they were little boys they had heard the Tlingit legend of the Kushtaka. If you are lost or injured in the Alaska wildlands, you'll be approached by a man or a group of men. They'll seem very friendly and kind, like kinsmen who are there to help you. Then they'll lead you to a safe place—at least they say it's safe. In reality, they bring you deeper and deeper into the unknown wilderness.

Gradually, the kind men transform into creatures that look like large otters. And they are evil. By the time you notice, it's too late. They will either tear you apart or turn you into a Kushtaka like them. Then your soul is trapped for eternity in an otter's body.

"I heard that Kushtaka make cries like a lost woman or a baby," one boy piped up. "You try to rescue them and the Kushtaka captures you."

"I haven't heard any babies crying," said another boy. "We're OK!"

"We should have brought my dog," said the boy whose house they'd been at. "Kushtaka are afraid of dogs."

"Hey, c'mon, guys!" another boy said. "It's just a story. Parents tell it to keep their little kids from wandering into the woods."

"Yeah," said the boy who lived there. "Anyway, it's freezing out here and it's almost three o'clock in the morning. Let's head home."

Quickly the group walked back, each boy looking intently into the woods, covering every direction, listening for anything odd. At last they reached the edge of the dense tree line and saw the house ahead, glowing warmly.

A baby's cry pierced the darkness.

In a dead sprint the group took off for the safety of the house. Once they'd made it into the yard, one of the boys turned around to look back at the forest. What he saw standing there was like no creature of nature.

About five feet tall, the thing stood straight up on its hind legs. It resembled an otter—but things were definitely not right. Large patches of thick brown fur covered its body. Wherever fur was missing, black, leathery skin shone through. Its almost humanlike hands were covered in the same black skin, with spindly, bony fingers that ended in large claws.

The thing held the boy's gaze, its head cocked to one side and its mouth twisted into an evil smile. Its teeth were long and sharp. Its eyes were a bright, burning yellow. With a wretched shriek, it fell on all fours and sprinted toward the group.

Clambering over one another, the boys closest to the house rushed inside and slammed the door shut. But one boy was still outside.

"Where is he?" shouted the boy who lived there. "He was right with us!"

Terrified, the boys crowded around the window. Just outside, they saw the boy who had stopped to look back. He wasn't calling for help or trying to get inside. He faced the woods calmly, as if frozen in place.

Then he was on the ground, the creature bent over him, its fangs and claws moving closer.

A loud bark shattered the night air. The boy's dog raced toward the beast, growling and snapping. The terrified creature sprang from the boy and galloped into the trees. That's when the boys inside knew they had been hunted by the Kushtaka.

Shouting with relief, they all raced out to help their friend. As he slowly rose and walked toward them, the boys saw it. His upper lip was split like an otter's and he reached out sharp, black claws toward them.

Deer Woman

TRADITIONAL PONCA LEGEND, TOLD BY DAN SASUWEH JONES, PONCA

Deer Woman's upper body is that of a woman, but she walks on the powerful legs and split hooves of a deer. Deer Woman has the strength of five men and runs with the speed of a deer. She is mystically ageless. She can appear out of thin air, mainly at night, some say, from an underground spring. Legend says that her quest is to find her dead mate, but it is an impossible pursuit. The frustration has led to madness. Few if any have seen her face and lived to tell about it; to gaze into her eyes will paralyze you and eventually kill you—possibly by taking control of your mind. If you are a husband unkind to his wife, you could disappear forever after her visit. Deer Woman is known to many tribes across America. From time to time she still menaces our Ponca tribe.

It was a hot August night in 1955, the third Saturday of the month, to be exact. The Ponca Powwow, a celebration of our culture, was in full swing. Hundreds of dancers—both men and women—wore colorful regalia wonderfully decorated with patterns from hundreds of years before our time.

Many more people were not dancing or wearing regalia, but were taking part as onlookers. As the clock approached midnight, the main event ended. The singers, dancers, and guests cleared the arena and the lights were turned off.

Now it was time for the young adults to have their turn to celebrate. Their time is called "the 49." The term is said to come from a time when fifty young Ponca warriors went off to war, but only forty-nine returned.

The 49 dance is held in the dark, in a large circle with a drum at the center. On this moonlit night, all the faces of the dancers and singers were illuminated. During a 49, everyone sings along to the songs, including the young people as they dance.

Two young people in love were dancing arm in arm, and the young woman kept noticing the woman dancing next to her. It was odd, she thought, that the other woman was dressed in a black skirt and her head was covered with a black shawl. Such clothes are a sign of mourning, and in the Ponca culture a person in mourning doesn't dance for a year after losing a loved one. Along with the black skirt and shawl, the woman wore a white ruffled blouse that had an old-time look to it.

Glancing down, the young dancer noticed that the woman's long black skirt covered her feet so well that even when the woman kicked out her skirt as she danced, her feet were never exposed.

That's funny, thought the young woman. *My skirt is the same length as hers, but I can always see my feet when I kick out.* Now she was really puzzled. Maybe the woman had very small feet?

The young woman went back to singing and dancing next to her boyfriend. When the song ended, she watched the woman in black. The woman was so covered up by the skirt and blouse that it was hard to tell her age. The woman walked off and sat on the bleachers alone.

Even though the arena lights were off, the moon washed the area with light. A young boy wandered by the woman in black, and he, too, noticed she was sitting there alone. He noticed how her head was bent forward and covered with the shawl. And he noticed that she was very different from everyone else.

As he gazed at her, his eyes followed her long skirt down to the ground. Then he saw it. One of her feet was exposed at last. It was shiny and black. He looked harder and saw it was the hoof of a deer, covered with black polish. The boy had heard the stories of her, and he began screaming at the top of his lungs: "Deer Woman! Deer Woman!"

In a flash her shawl dropped to the ground, and she stood up to face the boy. He froze as she towered over him and looked into his eyes.

Barely a moment passed before someone threw the switch to turn on the arena lights. Then several hundred young people stared at her in awe—and fear.

Right in front of her, the frozen child who'd called her name was so overwhelmed he could barely breathe. He watched as the black skirt dropped away and a white tail flicked behind the powerful body. Still wearing the white ruffled blouse, the Deer Woman was a woman from the waist up. From the waist down she stood on the two powerful hind legs of a deer. She looked out across the crowd with cold, black eyes.

At that very second dozens of young men started to run toward her.

"Killer!" they taunted. "Get her!" Many of them had lost relatives to the beast. Now was their time to get even. They closed in on her.

But she was faster. She turned and ran straight for the opposite set of bleachers, and in three bounds she leaped ten feet up and over them.

The young men tried to follow her. As they raced around behind the bleachers, they could not match her speed. She disappeared into the trees.

By the next day, many of our elders were aware of the previous night's events—and they were talking. One of them told Deer Woman's story.

Out of those fifty Ponca warriors who went off to fight, the young man who never returned had a beautiful Comanche bride. She had married the young Ponca man, and their life had been so happy. When he didn't return from war, she was filled with so much grief that they say she died of a broken heart.

No one knows what happened, but for some reason her ghost never crossed over. Her broken heart found a home in the chest of a creature half woman, half deer. She wanders Earth as Deer Woman, looking for her husband. But because he did cross over, they will never meet.

She has gone mad searching for him. Behind her she leaves a trail of death. They say she punishes any husband who is not as kind and respectful as her love, lost to her forever.

The Stikini

BASED ON A SEMINOLE TALE,
TOLD BY BROCK BATTENFIELD, SMALL TOWN MYTHS

*By day, a Stikini looks like an average person. But after dark, beware.
Its arms turn into wings and grow feathers; claws spring out from the
tips of its fingers. Its nose becomes a beak, and the large black eyes
of an owl peer out from a round, feathered face. Stikini, or Stigini,
and sometimes Ishtikini, is a supernatural shape-shifter of Seminole
legend—a witch by day that transforms into an owl by night.
When the United States government forced the Seminole tribe to leave
Florida for Oklahoma in the 1800s, the Stikini came with the people,
planting its powers in a new place out west. While transforming,
a Stikini remains as tall as a human until the final step: The creature
vomits up its heart, liver, and other organs and hides them, often leaving
them to hang from a tree or from the rafters of an abandoned building.
This allows the monster to shrink to the size of an owl. Then it finds
its prey—usually a sleeping human—and rips the heart out through
the mouth. Flying back to its shelter in the woods, it savors its feast.
As morning dawns, it retrieves and reinserts its organs.
Then it transitions back into the community.*

On a warm summer night in Oklahoma, friends dared a brother
and sister to go into an abandoned church that had been used
by Seminole Indians in the early 1900s. Now it stood dark and
foreboding.

The church wasn't far away—it stood at the end of the siblings' own gravel driveway—and the two kids knew the way, down to every last tree. But on that evening, the walk was long and dark. Shadows from the trees danced around them, and they smiled nervously.

But eventually, they came to the end of the path. They paused at the gate, for the churchyard was another matter. So confident when they started their walk, the siblings became more and more terrified at the thought of walking past the graves and into the church itself.

"That building is cursed," their dad had told them. "Stay far away from there."

With fluttering bellies the two slowly stepped onto the chipped flagstone walk that led to the church's main door.

Not a sound broke the stillness. Gaining courage, they walked up to the big oak door and pulled the ancient iron handle. It was locked. Taking a deep breath, they made their way around the side of the church and peered in through a broken window.

Something moved inside.

In a panic they joined hands and pulled each other back to the flagstone path, then to the gravel driveway. Stopping to catch their breath, they looked back at the church. Above the roof hovered a set of bright yellow eyes.

In seconds flat the siblings sprinted back to their house and screamed to the other children waiting in their yard: "It's there. The Stikini is there!" They raced inside and slammed their door.

The others laughed. "No way," they said. "Let's go take a look."

Halfway down the road, one child looked up to see a shadow hovering above them in the trees. "There!" she screamed as she pointed.

On a high tree branch sat a human silhouette, hovering. Then the monster spread its wings and released an ear-piercing screech.

In a shot the group took off, running back down the drive. They pounded on the door of the brother and sister's house. The father answered and pulled the children inside.

"What is going on?" he demanded. He sat quietly as the children spilled out the story of the church and the monster inside.

"Hmmm," he said, his brow knitted together. "My son and daughter didn't tell me. We told them to stay away from there. But now you've all seen it—the Stikini. It was probably hiding its organs in the church.

"You'd better stay here tonight," he continued. "It may be looking for you. I'll call your parents and tell them you're safe."

The children climbed the stairs to join the brother and sister, who were already asleep. Soon the house was quiet.

Outside, the Stikini hovered on a branch, its yellow eyes watching the settling house. As the last light flicked out, the Stikini raised its wings and swooped down toward an open window.

Warning

TOLD BY EUGENE REDSTEER, NAVAJO, ARIZONA

Among the Navajo and other Native American nations, it can be an
unlucky omen to hear a hooting owl. It may even mean death is nearby,
as the ancient Aztec and Maya believed. Owls are sometimes said to
carry messages from beyond the grave or to deliver supernatural
warnings to people who have broken tribal taboos. A howling coyote can
also mean trouble is up ahead. Sometimes evil medicine men turn into
coyotes at night to practice black witchcraft. They're called skinwalkers
or shape-shifters, and they're dangerous. Saying prayers and burning
cedar wood are strong protections against all these evils.
Bravery helps, too, as you'll find out in this story.

This happened back in 2014, around October. I work at a factory here on the Navajo Nation. There were only two of us working on this particular night on the evening shift—me and a woman. We got off work around about midnight. Outside, it was windy and raining hard. It was very dark. Together we walked back to our vehicles in the parking lot. The lot was big and mostly empty, and our cars were parked far away—at the other end. The wind picked up and howled around us as we made our way through the black night. Above the parking lot, massive power lines dipped and swayed in the gusts.

Just as we walked under one of the power lines, we heard it:

Hoooo—hoooo . . . an owl called above us.

A chill ran through me.

We both looked up and searched the lines dancing above us. It was too dark to see the owl, but we knew it was sitting on one of those power lines.

Hooooo—hoooo . . .

Then, as we continued walking under the line, something crazy happened. The owl called out my name—both my first and last names.

"Eugene . . . Redsteer."

The lady next to me freaked out.

"Oh my God!" she screamed. "Did you hear that? It's calling your name!"

"Eugene . . . Redsteer!" It called my name out again.

This time I'd had enough . . . I stopped and started yelling at it.

"Get out of here!" I shouted. "You are afraid of me, so you hide in the dark and call my name!"

I kept looking around, trying to find where the owl calls were coming from.

"I said I'm not afraid of you—whoever you are!" I shouted. "Show yourself, you coward!"

Just as I said that, the sky opened up, and it poured down rain—hard, like bullets.

Ooooowww! At the same time, coyotes started howling behind the building we had just come from.

"Help!" My coworker grabbed me and held on to me as tightly as she could—her nails dug into my arms.

Oooooowww! Now the coyotes were howling even louder.

In a flash, the lady took off, running to her truck. I watched as she jumped in, slammed the door, and tore out of the open gate. I was still standing back under the power lines—all alone.

Taking a deep breath, I walked calmly back to my truck, started it up, parked it outside the gate, then locked up the gate for the night.

All the way home I kept yelling at the owl and coyotes: "You cowards!

Get out of here! Don't follow me! You don't belong here!"

In the driveway I raced out of my car and into the house. Inside, I burned some cedar for protection, and I said a prayer.

Nothing ever happened.

Maybe they were just trying to scare me—but they didn't. Even if they had, I would never let them see my fear.

They feed off your fear.

Skinwalker

TOLD BY ART TRACY JR., NAVAJO, ARIZONA

My mom used to tell all kinds of stories to us when we were little kids.
But I remember this one because it was a scary story to me. She said
it was a true story that happened on the Navajo Reservation, a long time
ago—maybe back in the 1920s or '30s. It's about an evil witch we call a
skinwalker. A skinwalker is half person and half animal. It starts as a
medicine man or woman who use their powers of healing for good.
But for some reason they turn to evil. Not only do skinwalkers bring pain
and suffering to their enemies, but they can crawl inside a person's mind
and control them. Skinwalkers often look like anyone else during the day,
then at night they transform into creatures with glowing eyes. They can
run like the wind and easily track down a person. Skinwalkers appear
during the day, too—waiting and watching for their victims.

There was a Navajo guy working as a ranch hand for a rich Navajo who had a lot of horses, cattle, and sheep somewhere around the western part of the Navajo Reservation, in Tuba City, Arizona. One day the man decided to go home to see his relatives and to check up on his family in the eastern part of the reservation—somewhere past Shiprock, New Mexico. So he talked to his employer and asked to take leave.

Soon he was on his way to see his family. Early that morning the worker had fastened his pack onto a good horse and started off on his long journey home. He rode cross-country through rugged canyons, mesas, and open range. Somewhere along the way he stopped for a rest.

While he was resting, he spied an old, mangy coyote sitting on top of a hill not too far away.

The man took out his rifle, aimed, and fired. The coyote slumped over and did not move again. Then the man climbed up to see his kill.

As he reached the top of the hill, he could not believe his eyes.

What lay before him was the dead body of a young Navajo man with long hair. The top half of his body was human, and the bottom half animal. His upper body was painted with designs and his lower half was covered with the fur of a coyote.

He had shot a skinwalker. It must have been resting like he was when he shot it.

Now he got scared. He didn't know what to do with it. He walked around, and then he saw a deep crevice along the canyon's edge. So he dragged the creature's body to the cliff's edge and threw it off.

Thud. He heard the body land somewhere deep down in the dark crevice. As his fear grew, he knew he needed to distance himself as far as possible from the creature and the place.

Quickly mounting his horse, he rode over Black Mesa, across Chinle Valley, and up the big Chuska Mountains. He rode all day and into the night, pushing his horse to the limit. He finally made it across the Chuska Mountains and past Shiprock, New Mexico, to his relatives' home.

There he told the family what had happened to him. They listened, their fear growing.

"You must never go back to your employer," they told him. "You have to stay here. The relatives of the skinwalker will be looking for answers— and they'll be out looking for you!"

Filled with fear, the man took their advice. Then one day, after several months, the visitor felt safe enough to come out of hiding. He had heard there was a traditional healing Yei'bi'cheii ceremony happening near Shiprock. He decided to attend it.

When he got to the ceremony it was packed with people. Many were camping, and their wagons were parked here and there. On the central grounds, rituals with singing and dancing were being performed by healers wearing elaborate masks.

Just as the visitor was beginning to enjoy the ceremony, he saw an old Navajo man walking around among the crowds of people. This old man was talking loudly and making an announcement to anyone who would listen.

"My family is looking for a son who went missing a couple of months ago," he called out.

He told of his son's journey in full detail. He told where his son had last stopped, where he was last seen, and his last known destination. After that, he had gone missing. He never showed up at his next expected stop.

The visitor grew cold as he listened. Next, the old man described exactly the features of the young Navajo skinwalker's face. Then the old man described the area of the reservation where the visitor had shot it.

Next, the old man said: "There is one man who knows what happened to our son—and that man is here among you today!"

The crowd murmured and looked around uncomfortably.

"We are camped over there"—the old man pointed—"and we would like for you to come over to our camp and tell us what you know happened to our son."

The visitor knew the old Navajo man was talking about him.

He left the ceremony as quickly and quietly as possible and made his way home. There he stayed in hiding for many years.

He never went back to work for his employer, and he never again went over to the western part of the Navajo Rez. After many, many years in hiding, he finally told his story only to a few people he trusted.

Coyote and the Turkeys

TOLD BY DAN SASUWEH JONES, PONCA

My people tell stories from long ago about animals. Coyote is a famous trickster, a loner, always in trouble and getting himself into situations that backfire. Turkeys are a symbol of strength, showing the power of family. They are animals, it's true, but as you listen to the storytellers, you can't help but think they are really talking about us.

I was commissioned to build a bronze sculpture from one of our old mythologies. The story I chose was called "Coyote and the Turkeys." It goes like this:

Coyote befriended a group of turkeys by singing to them of their beauty. As he sang and played his hand drum, he convinced them to close their eyes as they danced to his song—so they could better hear the music. They did so, because it helped them concentrate on how beautiful they were. Meanwhile, as they danced around him, he secretly grabbed them one by one and pushed them into a bag. Suddenly, they caught on to what he was doing—and they were furious! Then he had to run for his life as they chased him, trying to kill him.

My sculpture would show Coyote sitting on a rock, playing his hand drum to the turkeys. The sculpture would be quite large: six feet from the base to the top of Coyote's head.

One early morning while working in my studio, I had thrown the doors

wide open so I could look out to see the nature around me. My studio is in a remote area of Oklahoma, on a large lake, and it is common to see deer and turkeys right on my property. But never a coyote.

The initial form of the statue was almost complete, and I decided to take a break to do some much-needed lawn mowing. With the studio doors wide open, I could easily see the statue of Coyote as I mowed. At six feet tall, the statue was the most visible thing in my studio. I wondered what the animals in the woods must have thought as they peered out or passed by—especially the turkeys. After all, Coyote was one of their archenemies. Then I laughed; after all, the animals most likely didn't care.

So, I went about mowing along the road in front of my house—a gravel road nobody uses but us and a neighbor who only comes in the summer. So pretty much no one was around—except me and the wildlife.

As I was mowing, I happened to look up. To my surprise, a coyote was walking straight toward me. He had just stepped out of the thick brush on the side of the road. And to my even greater surprise, a few seconds later, two turkeys came out right behind him. They stopped just thirty or forty feet in front of me. There they stood: Coyote side by side with two large turkeys.

I was in shock. I had never seen or heard of turkeys and coyotes being anywhere near each other. Now, to my greater surprise, the three were walking together, straight toward me, looking at me. My brain was crying out: *Where's my camera?* I didn't even have my cell phone with me.

But wait a minute: My mower was loud! Why were these wild animals walking toward me instead of fleeing for their lives? Next, the two turkeys turned up my neighbor's road and walked away. The coyote stopped and stayed there, just looking at me. Then it walked even closer. When it got within ten feet of me, all my feeling of wonder vanished.

Now I was worried. *Something is wrong with this coyote! He is not acting scared of me or this loud mower. Does he have rabies? Those animals aren't afraid.*

But he didn't look sick or crazed. He wasn't even acting funny. This was not normal at all. He was so close that I could see the color of his light brown eyes. He turned his head from side to side like a dog will sometimes do.

After a minute or so he slowly walked off. I watched him, and he watched me, as he retreated down the road and off into the brush again.

"I need to take a break after that!" I said to myself.

Driving the mower back up to my studio, I could see the sculpture of Coyote. A very strange thought crossed my mind.

"Could he really have stepped down?" I asked myself. "No! It's just a coincidence."

Later that day my neighbor pulled up while I was working on the statue. We greeted each other, and started to chat.

"Funny thing," he said. "I was looking out my window this morning, and a coyote went running across my front yard. It kept looking back at something as it ran, like it was scared.

"Then," he added, "I saw a flock of turkeys chasing him—darndest thing I have ever seen!"

I looked up at the Coyote statue. His ancient story had played out in real life.

Acknowledgments

I want to acknowledge all the storytellers of the Ponca Tribe of Indians of Oklahoma, in my lifetime, for instilling in me a rich tradition of oral communication refined from Ponca storytellers since time immemorial. In my travels, I would like to thank the other tribes and their members who I have heard and shared stories with and who allowed me to experience the beautiful traditional elements of their cultures. I thank my traveling companion, Brenda, from all those years ago. People like Floyd Tiny Man Heavyrunner, Chief of the Blackfeet Crazy Dog Warrior Society, helped shape my views of this world and others hidden. A longtime friend and teacher, he was a legendary storyteller, fluent in the Blackfeet language and guided by his grandparents, Alfred and Agnes Wells, who were Spiritual Medicine People. I know all are at peace together on the other side of this life now. I need to thank my own mother and father, Lee and Velma Jones, who were my first story teachers. It was their stories of the old ways that first influenced me to understand the wealth in history and the power of the art of communication through the spoken word. Also a special thanks to my wife, Antje, and our son Lio and daughter Diamond. As well as my son Buck and daughter Meka. A special thanks to Barbara Brownell Grogan for all the work she did on this book. Also to Kevin Mulroy and Olivia Valcarce for their editorial input and Carol Norton for her design. To Weshoyot Alvitre, Tongva, for her wonderful art. Greatest thanks to all those storytellers who contributed to this book. And to Scholastic for publishing these works to further the voice of American Indians. Most of all to the stories themselves, whose spirits are in fact alive.

—*Dan SaSuWeh Jones, 2020*

Living Ghosts and Mischievous Monsters: Chilling American Indian Stories would not have been possible without the contributions of so many talented storytellers and collectors who have shared tales both traditional and present-day. The author and editors would like to thank Lavonne Rodriguez, administrator for Ghost Stories of the Wind River, at facebook.com/groups/GhostStoriesoftheWindRiver, for her support in this project and for introducing us to several storytellers whose work appears in these pages: Luis Wicho Aguilar ("La Lechuza, the Owl-Witch"); Solange K. ("Pa Ki Sko Kan, the Bones"); Maggie Marie Miller ("Twin Child Was Arapaho"); Eugene Redsteer ("Warning"); Stephanie Slim ("The Dark Figure"); and Art Tracy ("Skinwalker"). Thank you also to Paul Burke, administrator for the website First People of America and Canada–Turtle Island, at firstpeople.us, for sharing traditional versions of "The Chenoo: The Cannibal with an Icy Heart" and "The Deserted Children"; to Laura Redish, administrator for the website Native Languages of the Americas, at native-languages.org/legends, for sharing access to many traditional ghost stories and her knowledge of the history behind them, including access to "The Lost Hunters" and the story behind the Skudakumooch'; and to Glenn Welker, administrator for the multilingual website Indigenous Peoples Literature, at indigenouspeople.net, who shared a traditional version of "The Mashpee Sailor" and to Samantha Hatch, who shared her own chilling version of this story, printed here. Thank you to storyteller Vernandria Livingston ("The Garage Sale") and Kyler Edsitty, her editor at the University of Arizona *Lumberjack* student newspaper, where her story first appeared (in time for Halloween 2019). To Brock Battenfield, whose website Small Town Myths at smalltownmyths.com, shares "myths, legends, and scary stories" from around the world, including the versions of "La Llorona," "The Stikini," and "The Kushtaka" published here. Thank you to Ellen Baumler, longstanding historian for the Montana Historical Society, whose story "Sleeping Buffalo Rock" appeared in her 2016 book *Ghosts of the Last Best Place,* published by The History Press, Charleston, South Carolina, and whose abridged version of "The Vampire of Sleeping Child Hot Springs" appears on the historical plaque near the Montana springs. To author, historian, and consultant Herman Viola, curator emeritus for the Smithsonian National Museum of Natural History and senior adviser to the National Native American Veterans Memorial at the National Museum of the American Indian, for his guidance on the project and for his contribution, "You Don't Live Here Anymore." And to student consultant William Albea at the University of Wisconsin LaCrosse, contributor to the *Catalyst* literary journal, whose ear for a suspenseful tale guided us throughout.

—*The Editors*

OTHER SOURCES

"Rock Baby": This story was based on a summary of the Kawaiisu tale in "The Supernatural World of the Kawaiisu," by Maurice Zigmond, 1977, in *Flowers of the Wind: Papers on Ritual, Myth, and Symbolism in California and the Southwest,* Thomas C. Blackburn, ed., pp. 59–95, Ballena Press Anthropological Papers, Socorro, New Mexico, out of print, but now at Open Library, at https://openlibrary.org/publishers/Ballena_Press.

"The Lost Hunters": This story, accessed through native-languages.org, was told to anthropologists at the University of Maine by Mrs. Solomon, on Nov. 14, 1962, and published in the University of Maine Folk Life Center collection *Northeast Folklore,* Vol. VI, "Malecite and Passamaquoddy Tales," Edward D. Ives, ed., Northeast Folklore Society, Department of English, University of Maine, Orono, 1964.

FURTHER READING

Books

Baumler, Ellen. *Ghosts of the Last Best Place.* The History Press, Charleston, South Carolina, 2016.

Bond, Ruskin. *Penguin Book of Indian Ghost Stories.* Penguin Books, New York, 1993.

Bruchac, Joseph. *When the Chenoo Howls: Native Tales of Terror.* Walker and Company, New York, 1998.

Bruchac, Joseph and Sally Wern Comport (Illus.). *Whisper in the Dark.* HarperCollins, New York, 2009.

Bruchac, Joseph. *Skeleton Man* and *The Return of Skeleton Man,* HarperCollins, 2006.

Esparza, Lupe. *Haunting Stories: Native American Tales on Reservations and Rural Areas.* Independent, 2018.

Fourstar, Jerome. *Ghost Stories: The Indian Reading Series: Legends and Stories of the Northwest.* Pacific Northwest Indian Program, Northwest Regional Educational Laboratory, Portland, Oregon, 1978.

Garcez, Antonio R. *American Indian Ghost Stories of the West*. Red Rabbit Press, Moriarty, New Mexico, 2010.

Gideon, Amos, and Darren Zenko. *Native American Ghost Stories*. Lone Pine Publishing International, Auburn, Washington, 2006.

Jennings, Joe. *Ghosts of the Buffalo Wheel*. Sam and Gunny K9 Adventure Series. Independent, 2018.

Millman, Lawrence, and Timothy White. *A Kayak Full of Ghosts: Eskimo Folk Tales*. International Folk Tales. Interlink Books, Northampton, Massachusetts, 2004.

Mullins, G. W., and C. L. Hause (Illus.). *Ghosts, Spirits, and the Afterlife in Native American Indian Mythology and Folklore*. Light of the Moon Publishing, Colorado, 2019.

Quinn, Drake. *Campfire Stories for Kids: A Collection of Scary and Humorous Camp Fire Tales*. Hope Books, 2019.

Websites
First People of America and Canada–Turtle Island
firstpeople.us

Indigenous Peoples Literature
indigenouspeople.net

Native Languages of the Americas
native-languages.org

Small Town Myths
smalltownmyths.com

Welcome to the Nest of the Snow Owl
snowwowl.com

About the Author

Former Chairman of the Ponca Tribe of Indians of Oklahoma and member of the Producers Guild of America, **Dan SaSuWeh Jones** is a filmmaker who has produced work for *Sesame Street,* NBC, TBS, and other national and international networks. He worked as an honorary Imagineer and consultant for the Walt Disney Company's Disney America theme park and as a field producer for the television miniseries *500 Nations,* produced by Kevin Costner. As a bronze sculptor, he was a finalist in the competition for the National Native American Veterans Memorial at the National Museum of the American Indian on the Mall in Washington DC. He holds a seat in the House of Warriors, a traditional Ponca Warrior Society. He was storytelling author and consultant for *National Geographic Encyclopedia of the American Indian History and Culture.*

About the Illustrator

Weshoyot Alvitre is an author and illustrator from the Tongva tribe of Southern California. She currently resides with her husband and two children on Ventureno Chumash Territory in Ventura, California. Her work focuses on Indigenous voices on projects from children's books to adult market graphic novels. Most recently, these include *Ghost River: The Fall & Rise of the Conestoga,* written by Lee Francis 4 and edited by Will Fenton; *At the Mountain's Base,* written by Traci Sorell; and the video game *When Rivers Were Trails,* for which she was art director. She enjoys spinning yarn and collecting antiques.